WUTHERING HEIGHTS

CONTINUUM CHARACTER STUDIES

WUTHERING HEIGHTS
CHARACTER STUDIES

MELISSA FEGAN

continuum

Continuum
The Tower Building   80 Maiden Lane, Suite 704
11 York Road   New York
London SE1 7NX   NY 10038

www.continuumbooks.com

First published 2008

British Library Cataloguing-in-Publication Data
A catalogue record for this book is available from the British Library.

ISBN: 978-0-8264-9345-3 (hardback)
978-0-8264-9346-0 (paperback)

Library of Congress Cataloging-in-Publication Data
A catalog record for this book is available from the Library
of Congress.

Typeset by Servis Filmsetting Ltd, Manchester
Printed and bound in Great Britain by
MPG Books Ltd, Bodmin, Cornwall

For Tom Casement and Sheila Smyth

CONTENTS

SERIES EDITOR'S PREFACE

This series aims to promote sophisticated literary analysis through the concept of character. It demonstrates the necessity of linking character analysis to texts' themes, issues and ideas, and encourages students to embrace the complexity of literary characters and the texts in which they appear. The series thus fosters close critical reading and evidence-based discussion, as well as an engagement with historical context, and with literary criticism and theory.

Character Studies was prompted by a general concern in literature departments about students responding to literary characters as if they were real people rather than fictional creations, and writing about them as if they were two-dimensional entities existing in an ahistorical space. Some students tend to think it is enough to observe that King Lear goes 'mad', that Frankenstein is 'ambitious', or that Vladimir and Estragon are 'tender and cruel'. Their comments are correct, but obviously limited.

Thomas Docherty, in his *Reading (Absent) Character: Towards a Theory of Characterization in Fiction*, reminds us to relate characters to ideas but also stresses the necessity of engaging with the complexity of characters:

> If we proceed with the same theory as we apply to allegory [that a character represents one thing, such as Obstinate in Bunyan's *Pilgrim's Progress*], then we will be led to accept that Madame Bovary 'means' or 'represents' some one essence or value, however complex that essence may be. But perhaps, and more likely, she is many things, and perhaps some of them

lead to her character being incoherent, lacking unity, and so on. [. . .] It is clearly wrong to say, in a critical reading, that Kurtz, for example, in Conrad's *Heart of Darkness* represents evil, or ambition, or any other one thing, and to leave it at that; nor is Jude a representative of 'failed aspirations' in Hardy's *Jude the Obscure*; nor is Heathcliff a representation of the proletariat in Emily Brontë's *Wuthering Heights*, and so on. There may be elements of truth in some of these readings of character, but the theory which rests content with trying to discover the singular simple essence of character in this way is inadequate [. . .] (1983, p. xii)

King Lear, for example, is complex, so not easily understandable, and is perhaps 'incoherent, lacking unity'; he is fictional, so must be treated as a construct; and he does not 'mean' or 'represent' one thing. We can relate him to ideas about power, control, judgement, value, sovereignty, the public and the private, sex and sexuality, the body, nature and nurture, appearance, inheritance, socialization, patriarchy, religion, will, blindness, sanity, violence, pessimism, hope, ageing, love, death, grief – and so on.

To ignore this, and to respond to Lear as if he is a real person talking ahistorically, means we simplify both the character and the play; it means, in short, that we forget our responsibilities as literary critics. When, for example, Lear cries, 'Howl, howl, howl, howl! O, you are men of stones!' (5.2.255), it would be wrong to ignore our emotional response, to marginalize our empathy for a father carrying his dead daughter, but we must also engage with such other elements as: the meaning and repetition of 'Howl' (three howls in some editions, four in others); the uncertainty about to whom 'you are men of stones' is directed; what 'men of stones' meant to Shakespeare's audience; the various ways in which the line can be said, and the various effects produced; how what Lear says relates to certain issues in the play and introduces new ideas about being human; what literary critics have written about the line; and what literary theorists have said, or might say, about it.

When we embrace the complexity of character, when we undertake detailed, sensitive critical analysis that acknowledges historical context, and literary criticism and theory, and when we relate characters to themes, issues and ideas, the texts we study blossom, beautifully and wonderfully, and we realize that we have so much more to say about them. We are also reminded of why they are worthy of study, of why they are important, of why they are great.

Ashley Chantler
University of Chester, UK

AN OVERVIEW OF *WUTHERING HEIGHTS*

The popularity of *Wuthering Heights* as a text for undergraduate study is unsurprising given its enigmatic protagonists. But some students find it difficult to approach the novel's characters in a sophisticated way; seminar papers and essays typically dwell on the relationship between Heathcliff and Catherine, or whether Heathcliff is tyrant or victim, but without getting to grips with Brontë's complex development of these characters. Students also often forget that this novel, which is stereotyped as a novel about doomed love on the solitary Yorkshire moors, is in fact peopled with a large cast of idiosyncratic characters, each of whom plays an important part in the plot. Engaging with these characters will allow students to come to a better understanding of the themes, issues and context of *Wuthering Heights*.

Readers and critics have been intrigued – and disturbed – by the characters of *Wuthering Heights* since the novel's publication in 1847. The earliest reviews registered, on the one hand, revulsion and distaste for the characters, their actions and their language; on the other, the mysterious power of the story and its protagonists. The reviewer of the *Literary World* saw himself as being strangely compelled to read against his will:

Fascinated by strange magic we read what we dislike, we become interested in characters which are most revolting to our feelings, and are made subject to the immense power, of the book. [. . .] In the whole story not a single trait of character is elicited which can command our admiration [. . .] and yet, in spite of this, spite of the disgusting coarseness of much of the dialogue, and the improbabilities and incongruities of the plot, we are spell-bound, we cannot choose but read. (Stoneman, p. 12)

This emotional response to the characters – 'dislike', 'most revolting', 'disgusting coarseness' – says a great deal about the expectations of readers in the late 1840s. In an age of conduct books instructing people how to behave in all circumstances, Victorian readers were used to reading novels with protagonists whose character traits 'can command our admiration', exemplary characters the reader might want to emulate. *Wuthering Heights* struck the early reviewers as markedly different; the *Britannia* reviewer in January 1848 suggested that its characters were: 'a striking contrast to those regular forms we are accustomed to meet with in English fiction. They exhibit nothing of the composite character. There is in them no trace of ideal models' (Dunn, p. 289). The reviewer in *Atlas* in the same month stated: 'There is not in the entire *dramatis personae* a single character which is not utterly hateful or thoroughly contemptible' (Dunn, p. 283). The lack of the usual wholesome moral guidance and 'ideal models' in *Wuthering Heights* was puzzling to early readers; some even suggested this lack could make the book potentially dangerous.

Even Emily Brontë's sister Charlotte voiced her concerns about the impact of the characters on the reader; in her Preface to the 1850 edition of *Wuthering Heights*, after Emily's death, Charlotte tried to neutralize and apologize for the disturbing aspects of the novel by suggesting that Emily was not conscious of what she was doing. 'Where delineation of human character is concerned,' said Charlotte, 'I am bound to avow that she had scarcely more practical knowledge of the peasantry amongst whom she lived, than a nun has of the country people who sometimes pass her convent gates' (p. li). According to Charlotte, this innocent, reclusive parson's daughter had been overly impressed by the 'tragic and terrible' stories she had heard of these people's lives, and the result was *Wuthering Heights*: 'Her imagination, which was a spirit more sombre than sunny, more powerful than sportive, found in such traits material whence it wrought creations like Heathcliff, like Earnshaw, like Catherine. Having formed these beings, she did not know what she had done' (p. lii). Charlotte tries desperately to make *Wuthering Heights* fit the mould of the Victorian novel of exemplary types: 'For a specimen of true benevolence and homely fidelity, look at the character of Nelly Dean; for an example of constancy and tenderness, remark that of Edgar Linton' (p. lii). But even she can do nothing with Heathcliff, who 'stands unredeemed', a Satanic figure from whom the reader should rightly shrink, and whom even Charlotte cannot forgive Emily for creating: 'Whether it is right or advisable to create things like Heathcliff, I do not know: I scarcely think it is' (p. liii). The language here is a reminder of Victorian orthodoxy – authors must be cautious, considering whether it is 'right', or 'advisable', to create 'things like Heathcliff'; it is no wonder that this novel is frequently compared with Mary Shelley's *Frankenstein* (1818), as Emily emerges from Charlotte's preface as a Victor Frankenstein who has unleashed the monstrous Heathcliff on an unsuspecting public, perhaps for noble reasons, but with devastating consequences.

Charlotte's depiction of Emily as an innocent recluse, ignorant of human nature and therefore incapable of producing convincing characters, was very influential, partly because there is comparatively little evidence about Emily Brontë's life. Charlotte, who outlived her siblings, published more and corresponded widely, and has left a substantial record, but the most recent biographer of the Brontës, Juliet Barker, has said of Emily and her sister Anne: 'The known facts of their lives could be written on a single sheet of paper; their letters, diary papers and drawings would not fill two dozen' (1995, p. xviii). Certainly Charlotte's suggestion that their home town, Haworth, was 'a remote district where education had made little progress' ('Biographical Notice', p. xliv) owed more to what she knew London readers imagined Yorkshire to be than reality; Barker notes Haworth was not 'a remote and obscure village where nothing ever happened' but 'a township, a small, industrial town in the heart of a much larger chapelry, where politics and religion were hotly disputed and culture thrived' (1995, p. xix). What is clear from her only novel,

3

Wuthering Heights, is that Emily Brontë was very familiar with contemporary theories about character, identity and psychology; she was much more knowing than Charlotte's portrayal allows.

Take for instance Nelly Dean's comments on Heathcliff's sanity towards the end of his life: 'as to his reason, from childhood, he had a delight in dwelling on dark things, and entertaining odd fancies – he might have had a monomania on the subject of his departed idol; but on every other point his wits were as sound as mine' (p. 324). The term 'monomania' is chosen very carefully by Brontë; James Cowles Prichard (following the inventor of the term, Jean Etienne Esquirol) had defined it in 1835 as: 'partial insanity, in which the understanding is partially disordered or under the influence of some particular illusion, referring to one subject, and involving one train of ideas, while the intellectual powers appear, when exercised on other subjects, to be in a great measure unimpaired' (Taylor and Shuttleworth, pp. 252–3). By the mid-nineteenth century, when Brontë was writing her novel, 'monomania' was a frequently used term, and had come to mean 'almost any kind of irrational obsession' (Taylor, p. 47), but Brontë uses it in its precise original meaning; in spite of the constant questioning of Heathcliff's sanity by many of the other characters, Brontë makes it clear, through Nelly, that Heathcliff's mind is a complex organism, capable of being 'disordered' in one part (his obsessive love for Catherine), while 'unimpaired' generally. She also tracks this back to his past: 'from childhood, he had a delight in dwelling on dark things, and entertaining odd fancies'. The reflection of childhood in literature was relatively new; although the nature/nurture debate was obviously familiar to Shakespeare, it was the Romantics, notably Wordsworth, following on from philosophers of education such as Rousseau, who developed an understanding of the ways in which childhood acted as a crucible for the creation of character. Many Victorian novels adopted the form of the German 'Bildungsroman', or 'novel of education', in which we follow the protagonist from childhood innocence or ignorance to adult experience. Dickens's *Great Expectations* (1861), Eliot's *The Mill on the Floss* (1860) and Charlotte Brontë's *Jane Eyre* (1847) are good examples of novels where the central character is seen in childhood as essentially good-hearted but narcissistic, ambitious, or enraged, and dam-aged or traumatized by their upbringing; the protagonists learn through suffering. Emily Brontë understands that 'The Child is Father of the Man' (Wordsworth, 'My heart leaps up', l. 7), and takes care to show throughout the novel that her protagonists are heavily influenced by their childhood experiences; but unlike her contemporaries, she is less optimistic about the capacity for change and renewal through suffering.

Brontë also reflects the early Victorian interest in physiog-nomy, the pseudo-science of judging personality from facial fea-tures. Taylor and Shuttleworth note that: 'The cultural impact of physiognomy in England was diffuse [. . .]. One can trace in the novel, from the Romantic period onwards, a new focus on the details of physical form: vague references to a handsome or unprepossessing countenance are replaced by precise delin-eations of facial contours' (p. 4). Several of the characters in the novel seem to be keen physiognomists; Mr Linton suggests that Heathcliff's future of crime is mapped out in his face: 'would it not be a kindness to the country to hang him at once, before he shows his nature in acts, as well as features?' (p. 50). Nelly advises Heathcliff to change his dubious exterior by reforming his interior:

Do you mark those two lines between your eyes, and those thick brows, that instead of rising arched, sink in the middle, and that couple of black fiends, so deeply buried, who never open their windows boldly, but lurk glinting under them, like devil's spies? Wish and learn to smooth away the surly wrin-kles, to raise your lids frankly, and change the fiends to confi-dent, innocent angels [. . .]. A good heart will help you to a bonny face, my lad [. . .] if you were a regular black; and a bad one will turn the bonniest into something worse than ugly. (pp. 57–8)

Nelly believes that the face – and particularly the eyes (the clichéd 'windows of the soul') – reveal the hidden character; Heathcliff's sinking brows, lurking eyes and surly brow betray the evidence of the evil in his nature, as far as physiognomy is concerned. His face also betrays more: the suggestion of racial difference. Nelly's comment that even if he were 'a regular black' his face could be made attractive if his heart was good intimates the connection between physiognomy and negative racial stereotyping.

Another aspect of contemporary psychological enquiry reflected in the novel is the interest in dreams as reflections of the unconscious mind. We tend to associate the analysis of dreams with late nineteenth-century psychoanalysis; one of Freud's most important books was *The Interpretation of Dreams* (1900). But early nineteenth-century psychological enquiry was already acknowledging the insights provided by dreams; Robert Macnish noted in his *The Philosophy of Sleep* in 1830: 'It is undoubtedly owing to the faculty, sometimes possessed by sleep, of renewing long-forgotten ideas, that persons have had important facts communicated to them in dreams' (Taylor and Shuttleworth, p. 103). Lockwood, Catherine, Heathcliff and Nelly relate their dreams, and critics have been fascinated by how much their dreams reveal about the characters. Brontë emphasizes the importance of dreams by making her characters reflect upon them; Catherine says: 'I've dreamt in my life dreams that have stayed with me ever after, and changed my ideas; they've gone through and through me, like wine through water, and altered the colour of my mind' (p. 80). The dreams suggest hidden depths – sometimes (as in the case of Lockwood) so well-hidden and disturbing that the character cannot understand or accept them.

Wuthering Heights is also concerned with the extent to which origins and genetic inheritance shape character and identity. Again, the novel seems before its time; we associate this debate with Charles Darwin, who did not publish his *On the Origin of Species* until 1859, a decade after Brontë's death, but as with dreams and psychoanalysis, questions about origins and evolution surfaced long before the text with which they are now associated; Taylor notes: 'The concept of hereditary transmission was certainly not a new one at the beginning of the nineteenth century' (p. 64), and this was reflected in contemporary journals like *Blackwood's Magazine*, which was a favourite of the Brontë family. *Wuthering Heights* tracks three generations of Earnshaws and Lintons, and in the final generation in particular, in

6

Catherine Linton, Linton Heathcliff and Hareton Earnshaw, considers the extent to which their attributes are inherited from their parents. Stevie Davies suggests that the novel's central concerns include: 'genetic inheritance and conditioning; adaptation to environment; [. . .] the "improvement" of the stock (or its extinction) through generation and hybridization; competition between males for the female' (p. 54). Yet at the centre of this fascination with genetic inheritance is the orphan, Heathcliff. The figure of the orphan is not unusual in English literature, but it became commonplace in the Victorian period. Typically, the orphan is reclaimed at the end of the Victorian novel, discovers his or her origins and is reinstated in family and fortune: Jane Eyre, for example, finds her cousins and inherits a fortune from a long-lost uncle; Oliver Twist discovers who his parents were, inherits from his father, and is adopted by Mr Brownlow. But Brontë chooses to keep Heathcliff's origins a secret; we never learn who his parents were, where he came from, how much of his character was in his blood.

It is important to remember, however, that the characters of *Wuthering Heights* are literary constructs, and it is possible to trace Heathcliff's origins in earlier texts. Milton's Satan in *Paradise Lost* (1667) is a possible literary father, as are the doomed protagonists of Byron's poems *Manfred* (1817) and *The Giaour* (1813); like Heathcliff these are dangerously attractive anti-heroes whose terrible deeds are matched by powerful eloquence. The novels of Sir Walter Scott were a major influence on Brontë, including *The Black Dwarf* (1816), which includes characters named Earnscliffe and Ellieslaw, which Brontë perhaps echoes in Heathcliff and Earnshaw (Leavis, p. 32). Brontë was also an avid reader of German Gothic tales, such as those of Tieck and Hoffmann, and the Gothic paraphernalia of churchyards, graves, mysterious houses, vampires, ghouls and ghosts can be seen in her novel. The most important influence was Brontë's own earlier writings. The Brontë children (Branwell, Charlotte, Emily and Anne) had created two fictional worlds, Angria and Gondal, and devoted their childhood and early adulthood to writing the sagas of these lands; in fact Emily was still writing Gondal poetry when *Wuthering Heights* was published. Many elements of the Gondal

7

writings are evident in her only novel; the beautiful but cruel queen of Gondal, Augusta Geraldine Almeda, could be an early version of Catherine Earnshaw, but equally, in her long mourning for her dead husband, Augusta prefigures Heathcliff's grief for Catherine. The dark boy of sorrow, Amedeus, who loves his foster-sister but is destroyed by his passion for Augusta, could be another literary father for Heathcliff. Gondal provided a rich mine for the characters of *Wuthering Heights*. Juliet Barker asserts that: 'For Emily [. . .] without Gondal there was no writing. *Wuthering Heights*, which, ironically, is regarded as the archetypal Yorkshire novel, was actually Gondal through and through and therefore owed as much, if not more, to Walter Scott's Border country as to Emily's beloved moorlands of home' (1995, p. 501).

While Brontë demonstrates her familiarity with Victorian debates about the role of internal factors on identity – the conscious and unconscious mind, the genes – and acknowledges her debts to earlier fictional characters, she also engages with the external factors that shape character in fact and fiction. *Wuthering Heights* is located at the cusp of a new understanding about identity. Rick Rylance argues that we need to distinguish between 'the modern sense of character as the literary depiction of psychologically complex personalities' and the Victorian use of the term to mean 'a desirable moral quality' (Glen, p. 147), manifested by being religious, or gentlemanly or ladylike. To have 'character', in this sense, is to be acceptable to social orthodoxy, possibly by wrenching your psychological character to fit your exterior 'character'; this can be seen in Catherine's transformation into a lady following her stay with the Lintons, or her betrayal of her bond with Heathcliff in order to conform to the social demand that she marry well, or Heathcliff's understanding that to become powerful he must assume the 'character' of a gentleman.

While the novel registers this uneasy awareness of the complexity of both character (identity) and 'character' (reputation), for some critics there are no characters in either sense in *Wuthering Heights*. Early critics were divided over whether Brontë was right to create characters like Heathcliff; twentieth- and twenty-first-century critics disagree about whether the novel offers a psychologically convincing portrayal of character. Barbara Z. Thaden asks:

> Does *Wuthering Heights* even have characters? The characters are so similar that they seem to be mere parts of persons. The repetitions in plot emphasize the 'sameness' of all the characters, while famous statements like Catherine's 'I am Heathcliff!' add to the impression that these characters are strangely melded into each other. (p. 29)

Beth Newman suggests that *Wuthering Heights*, 'being firmly rooted in a Gothic tradition', treats character 'in terms of abstractions, in terms of general qualities or states of mind that are often rendered symbolically and obliquely, rather than through the kind of careful and explicit analysis of individual psychology that realistic novels offer' (Botting, p. 168). *Wuthering Heights* seems to straddle traditions and genres, combining the metaphysical aspects of Gothic characterization with what Nicholas Marsh has described as 'a grasp of psychology we would normally expect to find in a post-Freudian writer' (p. 70), or at least typical in nineteenth-century realism. Several names in the novel seem to hark back to eighteenth-century characterization, where names frequently reveal all there is to know about a man; 'Heathcliff', or 'Lockwood' are clearly emblematic, like Henry Fielding's use of the surnames 'Allworthy', 'Thwackum' and 'Square' in *The History of Tom Jones* (1749). Stevie Davies suggests that other names are anagrammatic: Catherine and Hareton contain 'heart' and 'earth', for example (p. 65). Mother and daughter share not only a first name (Catherine), but two surnames (Earnshaw and Linton), with the second Catherine's marriage to Linton Heathcliff adding the third surname her mother should have borne. Most notably, the characters remain essentially fixed; they lack the development typical of characters in realist novels, particularly in the 'Bildungsroman', where the protagonists are seen to learn from and be changed by the experiences they undergo. Beth Torgerson says: 'In fact, all of Emily Brontë's characters remain psychologically unchanged [. . .]. The psychological essence of each is static in this highly tumultuous novel' (p. 90).

Brontë provides metaphors of potential change: Catherine compares her love for Edgar to 'the foliage in the woods. Time will change it, I'm well aware, as winter changes the trees', but essentially her characters are closer to 'the eternal rocks beneath' (p. 82) which cannot be transformed. So while Brontë provides all the keys to understanding character we expect in a realist novel – childhood experience, genetic inheritance, a sophisticated approach to the conscious and unconscious mind, the forces of social expectation – she resists the anticipated change and growth that the realist novel demands. According to J. Hillis Miller, Brontë had to decide whether 'to bend the vision she had been expressing more directly and privately in the Gondal poems to the conventions of nineteenth-century fiction, or to bend those conventions to accommodate the vision' (p. 46). In *Wuthering Heights* she chose to bend the conventions of Victorian characterization rather than compromise her vision.

AN OVERVIEW OF *WUTHERING HEIGHTS: CHARACTER STUDIES*

The following chapters open with a consideration of two characters who are relatively peripheral to the events of *Wuthering Heights*, yet extremely influential to the reader's conception and understanding of the protagonists: Mr Lockwood and Nelly Dean. Brontë's decision to tell the story from two diverse points of view – the written account of the mystified outsider Lockwood and the oral account of the well-informed but prejudiced insider Nelly – has far-reaching consequences for the interpretation of the novel. Issues of identity, origin and heritage are pervasive in *Wuthering Heights*, a novel obsessed with duality and repetition, so following this examination of the narrative structure in Chapter 1, subsequent chapters will analyse the ways in which Brontë develops her insights into the psychology of individual characters by revealing how the actions of the previous generation impact upon and shape their descendants. Chapter 2 considers the first generation of Earnshaws and Lintons: Mr and Mrs Earnshaw (father and mother of Hindley and Catherine), Mr and Mrs Linton (father and mother of Edgar and Isabella) and the Earnshaws' servant Joseph. Chapter 3 examines the second generation of the same families: Hindley Earnshaw, and Edgar and Isabella Linton. However, since Heathcliff and Catherine deserve special consideration, detailed analysis of their characters is delayed until Chapter 4. The final chapter deals with the last generation, consisting of Catherine Linton and her cousins Linton Heathcliff and Hareton Earnshaw.

Note on the edition used
All quotations from *Wuthering Heights* are from the 2003 Penguin edition edited by Pauline Nestor.

CHAPTER 1

THE NARRATORS

One of the ways in which Brontë bends the conventions of nineteenth-century literature is in her use of multiple narrators. The entire novel is supposed to be the diary of Mr Lockwood; this forms a 'frame' narrative into which are embedded a range of other narrative voices, most notably that of Nelly Dean, who relates most of the story, but including reported speech from other characters, such as Heathcliff, Isabella and Zillah, and written testimony, such as Catherine's marginal comments in her books, or Isabella's letter to Nelly. This narrative structure looks back to earlier texts, such as the eighteenth-century epistolary novel (or novel in letters) as used by Samuel Richardson, Tobias Smollett and Fanny Burney. Mary Shelley's *Frankenstein* (1818) also uses this form; the entire novel is related in a series of letters from Robert Walton to his sister Margaret. The use of the 'frame' and 'embedded' narratives provides the reader with a rich diversity of points of view, but the lack of an omniscient third-person narrator who can tell us exactly what to think of characters and events is an important feature of the novel. Instead, we have two opinionated, but not always reliable, narrators: Mr Lockwood and Nelly Dean.

MR LOCKWOOD

That Lockwood is an utter contrast in personality, habits and experience to the other characters in the novel quickly becomes evident to the reader. Most of the characters have lived their entire lives on the moors, but Lockwood is an outsider, and views the north of England as an exotic hinterland, a temporary residence before he returns to the real world. Lockwood considers Catherine Heathcliff to be 'buried alive', and informs Heathcliff that 'many could not imagine the existence of happiness in a life of such complete exile from the world as you spend' (p. 13); clearly for Lockwood 'the world' is London, while Yorkshire is only exile from the world. When Lockwood announces he is leaving the Grange, Heathcliff shrewdly comments: 'Oh, indeed! you're tired of being banished from the world, are you?' (p. 304). The words 'exile' and 'banished' also suggest that residence in the North is a punishment for some sin; Lockwood feels he has been expelled from his native land (the South) against his will. Indeed, Lockwood's exile at Thrushcross Grange is a form of punishment for his loss of 'character', in Victorian moral terms; he has 'gained the reputation of deliberate heartlessness', he explains, in his treatment of a young woman the previous summer:

> While enjoying a month of fine weather at the sea-coast, I was thrown into the company of a most fascinating creature, a real goddess, in my eyes, as long as she took no notice of me. I 'never told my love' vocally; still, if looks have language, the merest idiot might have guessed I was over head and ears: she understood me, at last, and looked a return – the sweetest of all imaginable looks – and what did I do? I confess it with shame – shrunk icily into myself, like a snail, at every glance retired colder and farther; till, finally, the poor innocent was led to doubt her own senses, and, overwhelmed with confusion at her supposed mistake, persuaded her mamma to decamp. (p. 6)

Lockwood's language reveals his naivety and inexperience in matters of love; he describes the object of his attentions in clichéd terms as 'a most fascinating creature, a real goddess', while falling in love is being 'over head and ears'. He also alludes to Shakespeare's *Twelfth Night*; Viola, who is in love with Orsino, but cannot reveal it because she is disguised as the male Cesario, tells Orsino of her 'sister' (really herself), who pined to death because she was unable to speak of her love:

> She never told her love,
> But let concealment, like a worm i'th' bud,
> Feed on her damask cheek. (2.4.110–12)

The allusion is ironic; Lockwood represents himself in the passive role usually assigned to the female, but there is no obstacle to Lockwood telling his love beyond his own coldness – he 'shrunk icily into myself, like a snail'. The damage of Lockwood's concealment will be to the woman rather than himself; she has been 'compromised', put in a situation where her own reputation is called into question, which could have serious consequences for a woman in the nineteenth century. Lockwood's reaction and the language he uses to describe it mark him out as cold and unmanly – and extremely unlikely to understand the passionate characters whose story he is about to hear.

Lockwood's ideas about the North and the people who live there are equally naïve. The difference between the north and south of England was felt very powerfully in the Victorian period, as can be seen from the title of Elizabeth Gaskell's *North and South* (1855), where the South is characterized as cultured, leisurely and well-off, the North as dirty, industrialized and poverty-stricken. But it is important to remember that *Wuthering Heights* opens in 1801, and Brontë may be reflecting through Lockwood the influence of the Romantic view of northern landscapes as sublime (for instance in the poetry of Wordsworth) which led to hordes of tourists invading the Lake District and other 'remote' areas of Britain. Wordsworth's depiction of 'ordinary' people (farmers, huntsmen, shepherds, leech-gatherers) in his poetry was seen as revolutionary; prior to this the heroes and heroines of fiction and poetry were more likely to be extraordinary figures such as aristocrats or highwaymen. In his Preface to *Lyrical Ballads* (1802) Wordsworth defends his decision to show these hidden lives:

> Low and rustic life was generally chosen, because in that condition, the essential passions of the heart find a better soil in which they can attain their maturity, are less under restraint, and speak a plainer and more emphatic language; [. . .] in that

condition the passions of men are incorporated with the beautiful and permanent forms of nature. (p. 597)

Lockwood also seems to recognize the value of 'ordinary' lives as less trivial, more vital than the lives of town folk:

I perceive that people in these regions acquire over people in towns the value that a spider in a dungeon does over a spider in a cottage, to their various occupants; and yet the deepened attraction is not entirely owing to the situation of the looker-on. They *do* live more in earnest, more in themselves, and less in surface change, and frivolous external things. (p. 62)

But Lockwood's metaphor exposes his negative view of the North: it is a 'dungeon' to the South's homely 'cottage'; if he is fascinated by the people of the North, it is only for want of other distraction.

Lockwood's habits mark him out as a fashionable, wealthy southerner. He is astonished that Nelly expects him to dine at 12 noon, when he is more used to eating at 5 p.m.; he rarely goes to bed before 1 am or 2 a.m., and gets up at 10 a.m., while the residents of Wuthering Heights retire at 9 p.m. and rise at 4 a.m. Nelly tells him: 'You shouldn't lie till ten. There's the very prime of the morning gone long before that time. A person who has not done one half his day's work by ten o'clock, runs a chance of leaving the other half undone' (p. 62). But Lockwood is clearly a man of leisure; the summer before the novel opens, he has spent a month at the seaside; at the end of the novel in September 1802 he calls on the Heights on his way to a shooting expedition in the North. He pays for a year's lease of the Grange, but only stays just over a month. Lockwood seems to have little conception that the Heights is a working farm; he arrives in the afternoon, and is mystified to find no one to greet him in the house, not considering the need to tend livestock. His class prejudices are clear in the way he describes Nelly. Initially described as 'a matronly lady taken as a fixture along with the house' (p. 9), and 'My human fixture' (p. 31), Nelly is merely a piece of furniture in Lockwood's eyes. When he begins to question her about the Heights and the Grange, he fears that she will have nothing to tell but her own life story, which 'could hardly interest me' (p. 33). But while Lockwood has little in common with the characters whose story he records, he has much in common with the typical first reader of the novel, likely to be an educated, middle-class, town-dweller, and as ignorant of the lives of Yorkshire yeoman farmers as Lockwood.

His journey to the North, a place of exile, sublime landscape and passionate people is Lockwood's attempt to reinvent himself as the rebel he so clearly is not. Cates Baldridge comments that: 'Lockwood is [. . .] an example of the successfully socialized man who wishes he weren't, whose only genuine rebellion against the straitening ethical order he inhabits takes place in the realm of fantasy' (p. 278). He imagines knocking down Hareton for his insolence, or rescuing Catherine: 'What a realization of something more romantic than a fairy tale it would have been for Mrs Linton Heathcliff, had she and I struck up an attachment [. . .] and migrated together, into the stirring atmosphere of the town!' (p. 304). But Lockwood is no knight in shining armour; his one rebellious action, stealing a lantern, leads to a catastrophic nosebleed which leaves him 'sick exceedingly, and dizzy and faint' (p. 18). He portrays himself as a misanthrope, 'exaggeratedly reserved' (p. 3), a loner – a kind of Byronic hero; yet he is desperate for society, forcing his way into the Heights and monopolizing Nelly's time. Lockwood cannot even make it through one day alone:

> I, who had determined to hold myself independent of all social intercourse, and thanked my stars that, at length, I had lighted on a spot where it was next to impracticable, I, weak wretch, after maintaining till dusk a struggle with low spirits, and solitude, was finally compelled to strike my colours, and, under pretence of gaining information concerning the necessities of my establishment, I desired Mrs Dean, when she brought in supper, to sit down while I ate it, hoping sincerely she would prove a regular gossip [. . .] (p. 33)

His lack of self-knowledge is compounded by his errors about other people. Lockwood narcissistically projects his own imagined character onto others. He describes Heathcliff as 'A capital fellow!' (p. 3), and attempts to read Heathcliff's character in the light of his fantasy of himself:

> possibly some people might suspect him of a degree of under-bred pride – I have a sympathetic chord within that tells me it is nothing of the sort; I know, by instinct, his reserve springs from an aversion to showy displays of feeling – to manifestations of mutual kindliness. He'll love and hate, equally under cover, and esteem it a species of impertinence to be loved or hated again – No, I'm running on too fast – I bestow my own attributes over-liberally on him. (pp. 5–6)

The first-time reader, not realizing how unreliable Lockwood's instincts are, may be fooled, but anyone who has read the novel understands how far Lockwood is from the truth; there is no one who engages in more 'showy displays of feeling' in the novel than Heathcliff, no one less likely to 'love and hate, equally under cover'.

On his second visit to the Heights, Lockwood makes a series of excruciating gaffes. First, attempting small talk with Catherine, he mistakes a heap of dead rabbits for cats. Then, using the hyperbolic language he mistakes for politeness, he compliments Heathcliff on his 'amiable lady [. . .] the presiding genius over your home and heart' (p. 13), not realizing that Heathcliff's much-hated wife, Isabella, is long gone, and now dead. Disabused of his notion that Catherine is Heathcliff's wife – a thought that is repulsive to both – he next decides that Hareton – whom he had thought a servant, and now assumes is Heathcliff's son – is the 'favoured possessor of the beneficent fairy' (p. 14). Lockwood has blundered into the hornets' nest of tormented relationships at the Heights, and has no idea how to remedy his situation: 'I began to feel unmistakably out of place in that pleasant family circle. [. . .] I resolved to be cautious how I ventured under those rafters a third time' (p. 14).

Lockwood emerges from these scenes a comic figure, and Brontë could have chosen to leave him at that; but she complicates him dramatically by exposing the darker side of his psyche in his dreams. Put to bed in the room that Heathcliff and Catherine shared as children, Lockwood entertains himself by reading Catherine's scratched inscriptions on the ledge and her marginal comments in her library; the diary-writer becomes diary-reader, attempting to 'decypher her faded hieroglyphics' (p. 20). Catherine's record of her and Heathcliff's rebellion against the tyranny of Joseph and Hindley is written in the margins of a religious book, 'Seventy Times Seven, and the First of the Seventy First. A Pious Discourse delivered by the Reverend Jabes Branderham, in the Chapel of Gimmerden Sough'. Lockwood has a dream in which a number of issues combine: Catherine's objections to Joseph's long sermon; Lockwood's awareness of the real chapel, which has Gothic overtones: 'I have passed it really in my walks, twice or thrice: it lies in a hollow, between two hills – an elevated hollow – near a swamp, whose peaty moisture is said to answer all the purposes of embalming on the few corpses deposited there' (p. 23); Lockwood's guilt over his rejection of his 'goddess'; and his thwarted rage at his treatment by Heathcliff.

Lockwood dreams that Joseph is guiding him through the snow. Joseph's 'pilgrim's staff' is actually 'a heavy-headed cudgel', revealing Joseph's use of religion as an instrument of power and control over the inhabitants of the Heights. Lockwood knows that either he, Joseph, or Jabes Branderham has committed the 'First of the Seventy First', the most heinous sin, and is about to be 'publicly exposed and excommunicated' (p. 23). They arrive at the chapel, where Lockwood is dismayed to find that Branderham is preaching a sermon 'divided into *four hundred and ninety* parts [. . .] each discussing a separate sin!' (p. 23). Having 'writhed, and yawned, and nodded, and revived' (p. 23) through 490 parts, Lockwood can take it no longer; he rises and denounces Branderham as 'the sinner of the sin that no Christian need pardon': 'Fellow martyrs, have at him! Drag him down, and crush him to atoms, that the place which knows him may know him no more!' (p. 24). '*Thou art the Man!*' replies Jabes, ordering the congregation to 'execute upon [Lockwood] the judgment written!' (p. 24); Lockwood, assailed by all, tries to grab Joseph's weapon (just as he had tried to steal the lantern earlier), but finds that blows aimed at him by the rest of the congregation fall on other heads instead. He wakes, relieved to find the 'loud taps on the boards of the pulpit' had actually been the branch of a fir tree touching the lattice.

The sermon is a reflection on forgiveness; in Matthew 18:21–2, Peter asks Jesus: 'how oft shall my brother sin against me, and I forgive him? till seven times?' Jesus replies: 'I say not unto thee, Until seven times but, Until seventy times seven'. This is generally understood to mean that one should always be merciful; no matter how many times a person has sinned, one should continue to forgive. But the sermon has taken the text literally: one should forgive 490 times, but the 491st time is unpardonable and must be punished. Notably, the first to lack mercy is not the religious bigot Joseph, or preacher Branderham, but Lockwood, who urges others to 'Drag [Branderham] down, and crush him to atoms'; he is unwilling to enact the violence himself, but not averse to witnessing it and enjoying it, in dreams and reality. Lockwood is clearly attracted to Catherine but afraid of her, and resentful of the temptation she represents. He warns himself to 'beware of the fascination that lurks in Catherine Heathcliff's brilliant eyes' (p. 153), and admits to Nelly: 'It may be very possible that *I* should love her; but would she love me? I doubt it too much to venture my tranquillity, by running into temptation' (p. 256). Before returning to the 'busy world', he witnesses an argument between Hareton and Catherine. Turning his back 'from a gentlemanly idea of relieving [Hareton's] embarrassment', he hears, 'not altogether disapprovingly, a manual check given to her saucy tongue'; when he turns, Catherine is 'sucking her damaged lip' (pp. 302–3). Lockwood's 'gentlemanly' behaviour has resulted in Hareton slapping Catherine, and Lockwood approves; he gains a vicarious revenge against Catherine for her obvious lack of interest in him.

It is also significant that Lockwood associates Branderham with Heathcliff: 'Was not the Reverend Jabes Branderham akin to you on the mother's side?' he asks (p. 27). Heathcliff had earlier insulted Lockwood by suggesting he could not be trusted alone in the house, and had mocked and laughed at him through his errors and sickness; in his dream Lockwood sees Branderham as Heathcliff's proxy, and seeks to 'crush him to atoms'. This is complicated by the fact that Lockwood has associated Heathcliff with himself – 'I bestow my own attributes over-liberally on him' (p. 6) – so the attack rebounds, and Lockwood finds himself accused of the unpardonable sin. At the start of the dream, Lockwood had thought Joseph was guiding him home, but as he had revealed early in the novel: 'my dear mother used to say I should never have a comfortable home, and only last summer, I proved myself perfectly unworthy of one', in his actions to the young lady at the sea coast (p. 6). Instead of being taken to a 'comfortable home', he is taken to a Gothic chapel to be exposed and excommunicated.

This dream is disturbing enough, but the dream which follows is terrifying, and has been the subject of much speculation among critics. 'But why should Lockwood, the well-mannered urbanite, dream *this*?' asks Dorothy Van Ghent (Allott, p. 177). Perhaps it is because Brontë means Lockwood to be more than simply a 'well-mannered urbanite', or to signal that even a 'well-mannered urbanite' can feel rage and fear, and act with extreme cruelty. Lockwood dreams that he has smashed the glass in the casement to reach the fir tree branch, but when he reaches out his fingers close 'on the fingers of a little, ice-cold hand' (p. 25); a 'most melancholy voice', identifying itself as 'Catherine Linton' cries: 'Let me in – let me in! [. . .] I'm come home, I'd lost my way on the moor! [. . .] twenty years, I've been a waif for twenty years!' (p. 25). Lockwood reacts violently:

> As it spoke, I discerned, obscurely, a child's face looking through the window – Terror made me cruel; and, finding it useless to attempt shaking the creature off, I pulled its wrist on to the broken pane, and rubbed it to and fro till the blood ran down and soaked the bed-clothes: still it wailed, 'Let me in!' and maintained its tenacious gripe, almost maddening me with fear. (p. 25)

Lockwood piles the books in a pyramid to prevent the child from getting through the window, but they are thrust forward; Lockwood yells and wakes.

Lockwood's attempt at interpreting his dream – 'Alas, for the effects of bad tea and bad temper! what else could it be that made me pass such a terrible night?' (p. 22) simply will not do; this dream has been the focus of critical attention from the outset because it resists such easy explanation. The child on the moors for 20 years has perhaps been suggested by Lockwood's reading of Catherine's 'scamper on the moors' with Heathcliff, which was 'dated some quarter of a century back' (p. 20). But as Lockwood himself notes, the naming of the child is odd: 'why did I think of *Linton*? I had read *Earnshaw* twenty times for Linton' (p. 25). He also seems to associate the child obscurely with sin; when he wakes, he describes her as 'the little fiend [. . .] that minx [. . .] she must have been a changeling, wicked little soul! She told me she had been walking the earth these twenty years: a just punishment for her mortal transgressions, I've no doubt!' (p. 27). The spectre is feminized by his conscious mind, but it is notable that in the dream, Lockwood does not seem to recognize the child's gender, using 'it' rather than 'her' throughout. For Ronald R. Thomas, the child represents both Lockwood's past and his repressed sexual desires:

> Lockwood 'must stop' Catherine's request for admission because it represents forces he believes he must deny. Most obviously, the dream figures his refusal to permit passion and intimacy into his life. The bloody scene of penetration and exclusion manifests a desire for erotic experience which is overcome by a repressive fear of it. This violent exclusion of the female figure from his bed recalls the attraction Lockwood has already admitted for the younger Cathy Linton and the failed love affair from which he has recently fled. But in a deeper sense, to shut out the child at his window is to shut out his own past, the 'me' Lockwood will not let in. (pp. 119–20)

He attempts to do this with books, piling them up against the incursion of these repressed fears and urges, using them 'to create a protective buffer between himself and the forces of his unconscious' (Thomas, p. 120). Books represent security and control for Lockwood; he tells the younger Catherine: 'take my books away, and I should be desperate!' (p. 301). In spite of his desire to release his inner demons – signalled consciously in his romantic illusions about himself as a solitary misanthrope and unconsciously in his tormented dreams – he shores up his mind against the possibility of release with culture, education and reason. His response to Heathcliff's passionate grief is typical:

> I stood still, and was witness, involuntarily, to a piece of super-stition on the part of my landlord, which belied, oddly, his apparent sense [. . .] my compassion made me overlook its folly, and I drew off, half angry to have listened at all, and vexed at having related my ridiculous nightmare, since it pro-duced that agony; though *why*, was beyond my comprehen-sion. (p. 29)

Heathcliff's emotion is dismissed as 'superstition' and 'folly'; Lockwood is angry with himself for producing it, because his instinct is to ignore and draw away from deep feeling; once again he 'shrunk icily into [him]self, like a snail'. Heathcliff's mourning will remain 'beyond [his] comprehension'.

To an extent, perhaps, Lockwood is himself the 'protective buffer' between the protagonists and the reader. He is much closer in education, social background and experience to the typical first reader of *Wuthering Heights* than any of the other characters. While Wordsworth's farmers and shepherds are 'ordi-nary' in the sense of not being exceptional – heroic, handsome, wealthy, aristocratic – Lockwood is 'ordinary' in the sense of being a recognizable type of relatively young, relatively well-off, aimless middle-class urban gentleman. Lockwood would not be out of place in a nineteenth-century realist novel, and as the Gothic, supernatural elements of the plot are filtered through him, his emotional detachment from the story and allegiance to civilization and reason dilute them, and make them somehow more plausible. But, while readers may initially associate them-selves with Lockwood, his evident unreliability makes his inter-pretations suspect, and his attempts to render the uncanny acceptable fail. He emerges at the end of the novel untouched and unchanged. His response to the transformation of Hareton and Catherine is envy; seeing the radiance of Catherine's face: 'I bit my lip, in spite, at having thrown away the chance I might have

had, of doing something besides staring at its smiting beauty'
(p. 308). Instead of showing himself opening, 'feeling very mean
and malignant, I skulked round to seek refuge in the kitchen'
(p. 308). He evades their happiness in the same way that he had
drawn away from Heathcliff's grief, and all strong emotion:

> I felt irresistibly impelled to escape them again, and, pressing
> a remembrance into the hand of Mrs Dean, and disregarding
> her expostulations at my rudeness, I vanished through the
> kitchen, as they opened the house-door, and so, should have
> confirmed Joseph in his opinion of his fellow-servant's gay
> indiscretions, had he not, fortunately, recognised me for a
> respectable character, by the sweet ring of a sovereign at his
> feet. (p. 337)

Lockwood tries to redeem himself against charges of 'rudeness'
or 'indiscretions' with money; having 'gained the reputation of
deliberate heartlessness' (p. 6) before hearing the story of love
thwarted by class prejudice and lives ruined by financial mis-
deeds, he now tries to assert himself as 'a respectable character'
with a sovereign. The 'remembrance' he gives Nelly is a result of
his forgetting the story he has just heard.

The end of the novel sees Lockwood standing by the graves of
Catherine, Heathcliff and Edgar, denying the possibility that the
ghosts of Heathcliff and Catherine now roam the moors:

> My walk home was lengthened by a diversion in the direction
> of the kirk. When beneath its walls, I perceived decay had
> made progress, even in seven months – many a window
> showed black gaps deprived of glass; and slates jutted off, here
> and there, beyond the right line of the roof, to be gradually
> worked off in coming autumn storms.
>
>   I sought, and soon discovered, the three head-stones on the
> slope next the moor – the middle one, grey, and half buried in
> heath – Edgar Linton's only harmonized by the turf, and moss
> creeping up its foot – Heathcliff's still bare.
>
>   I lingered round them, under that benign sky; watched the
> moths fluttering among the heath, and hare-bells; listened to

the soft wind breathing through the grass; and wondered how any one could ever imagine unquiet slumbers, for the sleepers in that quiet earth. (p. 337)

Through alliteration and assonance he attempts to impose tranquillity and harmony on the scene; the final words of his record (and the novel) are 'quiet earth', but this earth is clearly not quiet. This is a dynamic landscape: the kirk has changed dramatically in seven months, and the coming storms will wreak more damage. The marker of Catherine's burial is itself 'half buried', while Edgar's headstone is invaded by 'creeping' moss. Heathcliff's grave is 'bare' – a stark, raw image, rather than a 'quiet' one. Moths flutter, wind breathes – nothing is entirely at peace here. Lockwood remains deliberately blind to possibilities he cannot comprehend.

NELLY DEAN

Lockwood's deficiencies are compensated for by the second narrator, Nelly Dean. The two narrators seem complementary: one southern, middle-class male outsider who records in written form, and one northern, working-class female insider who tells the story orally. Nelly has access to most – but not all – of the important information; when asked about Heathcliff's history, she says: 'I know all about it; except where he was born, and who were his parents, and how he got his money, at first' (p. 35). Her understanding of the characters of the protagonists and her access to information are the result of Nelly's nebulous position in the family. Nelly had grown up with the children at Wuthering Heights: 'I was almost always at Wuthering Heights; because my mother had nursed Mr Hindley Earnshaw [. . .] and I got used to playing with the children – I ran errands too, and helped to make hay, and hung about the farm ready for anything that anybody would set me to' (p. 35). The fact that Nelly's mother had been Hindley's nurse is significant, as in eighteenth-century rural societies this relationship was a special one, and Nelly's mother would have been considered Hindley's foster-mother. Hindley and Nelly had been born in the same year, and would therefore have been nursed together. Nelly clearly feels a greater loyalty to Hindley due to her mother's role in his upbringing: 'I had been [Hindley's] foster sister, and excused his behaviour more readily than a stranger would' (p. 66). When she hears of Hindley's death, Nelly is devastated: 'ancient associations lingered round my heart; I sat down in the porch, and wept as for a blood relation' (p. 186).

As a result of her upbringing, Nelly occupies a grey area between servant and sibling, playing with the children, but also making hay and running errands. This upbringing helps account for some of Nelly's character traits. While Lockwood had initially dismissed her as 'a matronly lady', 'a fixture', a 'worthy woman', he soon comes to realize that she is far from typical of a woman of her class. While Nelly asserts that 'we are the same as anywhere else, when you get to know us', Lockwood disagrees:

> you, my good friend, are a striking evidence against that assertion. Excepting a few provincialisms of slight consequence, you have no marks of the manners that I am habituated to consider as peculiar to your class. I am sure you have thought a great deal more than the generality of servants think. You have been compelled to cultivate your reflective faculties, for want of occasions for frittering your life away in silly trifles. (p. 63)

Nelly's language, in particular, marks her out as different; apart from the odd 'provincialism' which would only be noted by Lockwood's southern ear, she speaks Standard English, like the children she was brought up with, rather than dialect, like her fellow servant Joseph. Compare Nelly's language with that of the housekeeper Lockwood finds at the Grange on his return in 1802: 'Whet, whoiver knew yah wur coming? Yah sud ha' send word! They's nowt norther dry nor mensful abaht t'place – nowt there isn't!' (p. 306) Nelly occupies an in-between space, understanding dialect perfectly, but speaking 'educated' English. Nelly explains:

> I certainly esteem myself a steady, reasonable kind of body [. . .] not exactly from living among the hills, and seeing one set of faces, and one series of actions, from year's end to year's

end: but I have undergone sharp discipline which has taught me wisdom; and then, I have read more than you would fancy, Mr Lockwood. You could not open a book in this library that I have not looked into, and got something out of also; unless it be that range of Greek and Latin, and that of French – and those I know one from another: it is as much as you can expect of a poor man's daughter. (p. 63)

Nelly rejects Lockwood's romantic illusions about remote, sublime landscapes instilling a less trivial outlook on life, and attributes her separation from 'the generality of servants' to discipline and education. She makes no great claims for her education: she has 'looked into' and 'got something out of' books rather than studied them, and can only recognize the difference between Latin, Greek and French; nevertheless, a 'poor man's daughter' would not usually have the run of a gentleman's library. Nelly is exceptional rather than ordinary.

Given the novel's concern with origins and genetic inheritance, Nelly tells us surprisingly little about her own family. We know she is the daughter of a 'poor man', but apart from that she does not mention her father at all. Her mother, Hindley's nurse, 'lived till eighty, a canty dame to the last' (p. 231), but Nelly makes no reference to her beyond this. The 'sharp discipline' which teaches her wisdom must have come from the Earnshaws and Lintons rather than her own family, but like Lockwood, Nelly often fails to learn from her transgressions. The first example of this, appropriately, is associated with the arrival of Heathcliff. Nelly initially dislikes Heathcliff as much as Hindley does, showing little compassion and some cruelty. Ordered to wash the child and let it sleep with Catherine and Hindley, 14-year-old Nelly disobeys:

They entirely refused to have it in bed with them, or even in their room, and I had no more sense, so, I put it on the landing of the stairs, hoping it might be gone on the morrow. [. . .] Inquiries were made as to how it got there; I was obliged to confess, and in recompense for my cowardice and inhumanity was sent out of the house. (p. 37)

Nelly is briefly banished for treating Heathcliff inhumanely, but is soon reinstated, and joins her foster-brother Hindley in his attacks on the orphan: 'Hindley hated him, and to say the truth I did the same; and we plagued and went on with him shamefully, for I wasn't reasonable enough to feel my injustice' (p. 38). Nelly may be acting out of loyalty to Hindley, but it is possible that she also resents the position Heathcliff has been accorded within the family; while neither she nor Heathcliff can ever really be Earnshaws, Heathcliff has taken precedence over Nelly by being given the name of a dead son.

Nelly's bullying of the child goes unpunished: 'my pinches moved him only to draw in a breath, and open his eyes as if he had hurt himself by accident, and nobody was to blame' (p. 38). In the end, it is not 'sharp discipline' but self-interest that changes Nelly's behaviour. When the children fall ill with measles, Nelly has to 'take on [. . .] the cares of a woman' (p. 38) in nursing them; she is impressed by Heathcliff's fortitude compared to the continual demands of Hindley and Catherine, but she is especially moved by the attention she receives for her care of Heathcliff: 'He got through, and the doctor affirmed it was in a great measure owing to me, and praised me for my care. I was vain of his commendations, and softened towards the being by whose means I earned them, and thus Hindley lost his last ally' (pp. 38–9).

Many critics have stressed Nelly's good qualities: for Charlotte Brontë she is 'a specimen of true benevolence and homely fidelity' (p. lii); for Q. D. Leavis she is 'the normal woman, whose truly feminine nature satisfies itself in nurturing all the children in the book in turn' (p. 28); Mary Burgan describes her as 'the generative figure in the novel, the nourisher of children' (Bloom, p. 140). But Nelly also frequently discloses another, less nurturing and nourishing side to her character, to such a degree that some critics have questioned her motives; James Hafley even labelled Nelly 'The Villain in *Wuthering Heights*' (Stoneman, p. 55). An early reviewer, Mrs Humphrey Ward, noted the 'absurdities and contradictions' in the characterization of Nelly: 'Nelly Dean is presented as the faithful and affectionate nurse, the only good angel both of the elder and the younger Catherine.

But Nelly Dean does the most treacherous, cruel, and indefensible things, simply that the story may move' (Bloom, p. 10). While Nelly is often 'faithful' and 'affectionate', she never presents herself as a 'good angel', but is quite open about her cruelty, impatience and lack of compassion. The 'treacherous, cruel, and indefensible things' she does are not mere plot devices, done so 'that the story may move', but facets of a complex character.

Far from being 'the only good angel [. . .] of the elder [. . .] Catherine', Nelly delights in tormenting her:

> I've had many a laugh at her perplexities and untold troubles, which she vainly strove to hide from my mockery. That sounds ill-natured – but she was so proud, it became really impossible to pity her distresses, till she should be chastened into more humility. [. . .] I've said I did not love her; and rather relished mortifying her vanity, now and then [. . .] (pp. 68, 71)

While Nelly has not learnt from her own 'sharp discipline', she seeks to chasten and mortify Catherine to teach her humility. Nelly forgives and pities Hindley and Heathcliff in spite of their actions (Hindley, while drunk, tries to make her swallow a carving-knife; Heathcliff imprisons her for five days), but she has little compassion for Catherine. Compare her reactions to their deaths: she weeps for Hindley 'as for a blood relation' (p. 186), and at Heathcliff's passing her 'memory unavoidably recurred to former times with a sort of oppressive sadness' (p. 335). But she does not grieve for Catherine: 'Far better that she should be dead, than lingering a burden, and a misery-maker to all about her' (p. 164).

When the younger Catherine is imprisoned and forced to marry Linton Heathcliff, Nelly is full of self-reproach:

> I seated myself in a chair, and rocked, to and fro, passing harsh judgment on my many derelictions of duty; from which, it struck me then, all the misfortunes of all my employers sprang. It was not the case, in reality, I am aware; but it was, in my imagination, that dismal night; and I thought Heathcliff himself less guilty than I. (p. 276)

While she absolves herself – 'It was not the case, in reality' – some of Nelly's 'derelictions of duty' have terrible consequences. Nelly claims she was unaware that Heathcliff was listening while Catherine confessed her engagement to Edgar, but she sees Heathcliff steal out at the point when Catherine said it would degrade her to marry him; instead of telling the truth, and allowing Catherine to reconcile with Heathcliff, Nelly merely says she thinks Joseph is returning with Heathcliff. When she finally tells Catherine 'that he had heard a good part of what she said', she still holds back the truth, telling 'how I saw him quit the kitchen just as she complained of her brother's conduct regarding him' (p. 83).

Nelly frequently conceals and twists the truth in this way; she tells Lockwood that when questioned about Linton Heathcliff by Edgar, 'I hardly knew what to hide, and what to reveal' (p. 264), and this is typical of the information Nelly provides to the other characters – and perhaps also to Lockwood. At times this is a matter of policy; having been criticized by Edgar for telling tales, she decides not to tell him that Isabella has eloped with Heathcliff, despite the fact that 'There was a bare possibility of overtaking them if pursued instantly'. Nelly remains silent: 'I saw nothing for it, but to hold my tongue, and suffer matters to take their course' (p. 131). Following her imprisonment by Heathcliff, she seeks to ensure that all blame is diverted from her: 'I said Heathcliff forced me to go in, which was not quite true' (p. 282). Had she been less concerned about her own self-interest, the horrors of Isabella's marriage could have been prevented, and Edgar might have realized that his daughter and nephew were not well-suited, and taken action to amend his will before it is too late.

Her most significant silence is over Catherine's illness. While Nelly considers herself to be doing her duty in telling Edgar about Isabella's dalliance with Heathcliff, she also takes delight in 'thwarting Mrs Linton's pleasure' (p. 110). Following the fight between Edgar and Heathcliff, which clearly spells the end of Heathcliff's access to the Grange, Catherine turns to Nelly for help. But Nelly's first concern is herself: 'She did not know my share in contributing to the disturbance, and I was anxious to keep her in ignorance' (p. 116). Nelly should be aware of the consequences of this dispute; the last time Heathcliff and Catherine were separated, Catherine fell 'dangerously ill', and the doctor warned on her recovery 'that she would not bear crossing much, she ought to have her own way' (p. 89). This time Catherine is also pregnant, but Nelly is entirely unmoved by her threat 'to break their hearts by breaking my own' (p. 116). Catherine, exasperated by Nelly's lack of compassion, cries: 'I wish you could dismiss that apathy out of your countenance, and look rather more anxious about me!' (p. 117). Nelly refuses to humour Catherine, believing she is faking and could control herself if she tried. After listening at the door to Catherine and Edgar's argument, Nelly is summoned by the bell: 'I entered leisurely. It was enough to try the temper of a saint, such senseless, wicked rages!' (p. 118). She tells Edgar to ignore Catherine's frenzy 'though I could not help being afraid in my heart' (p. 118). Nelly is complacent in the face of the breakdown of family life at the Grange: Isabella mopes, Catherine starves herself for three days and Edgar shuts himself in his library, while Nelly 'went about my household duties, convinced that the Grange had but one sensible soul in its walls, and that lodged in my body' (p. 120).

Even when she sees the state Catherine is in after three days locked in her room, Nelly cannot resist humbling her by suggesting that Edgar does not care, and is happy among his books: 'I should not have spoken so, if I had known her true condition, but I could not get rid of the notion that she acted a part of her disorder' (p. 121). She finally becomes convinced by Catherine's actions that she is truly ill, and begins to feel alarmed when she remembers 'the doctor's injunction that she should not be crossed' (p. 122), but is still lacking in sympathy, and is rough with Catherine when she pulls the feathers from the pillow:

'Give over with that baby-work!' I interrupted, dragging the pillow away, and turning the holes towards the mattress, for she was removing its contents by handfuls. 'Lie down and shut your eyes, you're wandering. There's a mess! The down is flying about like snow! (p. 123)

The pillow is treated with more care than her raving mistress. Nelly is typically preoccupied by the impact this state of affairs will have on her; she is determined not to be blamed for her part in Catherine's decline, and continues to try to protect herself when Edgar discovers the extent of his wife's illness, telling him 'but it is nothing' (p. 127).

In her delirium, Catherine appears to recognize something malign in Nelly:

> I see in you, Nelly [. . .] an aged woman – you have grey hair, and bent shoulders [. . .] and you are gathering elf-bolts to hurt our heifers; pretending, while I am near, that they are only locks of wool. [. . .] Nelly is my hidden enemy – you witch! So you do seek elf-bolts to hurt us! (pp. 123, 128–9)

But in spite of Hafley's depiction of Nelly as the villain of the piece, she is not actively evil; her sins are largely sins of omission, arising from her insecure social position and her indoctrination in notions of duty and 'character' (i.e. the moral code). To a certain extent, Nelly is at the mercy of her employers; when Catherine marries Edgar, Nelly wants to stay at the Heights with Hareton, but Catherine's needs take precedence, and Nelly is forced to go to the Grange: 'I had but one choice left, to do as I was ordered' (p. 89). Nelly persuades the younger Catherine to keep her first trip to the Heights secret from her father, 'insist[ing] most on the fact, that if she revealed my negligence of [Edgar's] orders, he would perhaps be so angry that I should have to leave' (p. 198). An eighteenth-century servant dismissed without a good 'character' (i.e. a reference) from her employer would be in a very difficult position.

Nelly is clearly aware that her place in the social hierarchy at both Wuthering Heights and Thrushcross Grange is precarious; she is not indispensable. This vulnerability, plus the exceptional nature of Nelly's upbringing as both part of the family and servant, explain the duplicity and duality in her character. She is both 'Nelly' and 'Ellen'; the former, informal name is used by her childhood acquaintances at the Heights, the latter, formal version by those at the Grange, or those who share the Grange's 'civilising' values, like Frances Earnshaw. Nelly is one of the few characters to thrive at both the Heights and the Grange. Her adaptability is a survival mechanism, but also a measure of her dispossession; she belongs to neither place, because neither place belongs to her. Instead, she chooses to align herself with social orthodoxy, becoming 'a supporter of the status quo' (Thaden, p. 85), fearful of the rebellious energy of Catherine and Heathcliff. Gilbert and Gubar assert that Nelly is 'a censorious agent of patriarchy' (p. 292) in her zeal to repress and neutralize the threat posed by protagonists; but Nelly, like Lockwood, is also careful to repress the threat posed by dreams and the supernatural.

Nelly certainly aligns herself with the values she associates with the Lintons. She tells Lockwood: 'Hareton is the last of them, as our Miss Cathy is of us – I mean of the Lintons' (p. 34); the slip reveals that despite her Earnshaw upbringing, Nelly now considers herself a Linton. Once she arrives at the Grange, Nelly's allegiance switches from Catherine to Edgar: 'My heart invariably cleaved to the master's, in preference to Catherine's side; with reason, I imagined, for he was kind, and trustful, and honourable: and she – she could not be called the *opposite*, yet, she seemed to allow herself such wide latitude, and I had little faith in her principles, and still less sympathy for her feelings' (p. 107). Similarly, she feels little loyalty to Heathcliff: 'His visits were a continual nightmare to me; and, I suspected, to my master also' (p. 107). Describing herself as 'a steady, reasonable kind of body' (p. 63), Nelly rates honour, decent principles, and sound common sense far above any qualities Catherine and Heathcliff might possess.

But sensible Nelly is easily shaken, and the more superstitious, instinctual side of her personality has to be repressed and silenced. One of her weak point is dreams, which she dreads with a fear that undermines her allegiance to rational orthodoxy. When Catherine tries to explain her love for Heathcliff by relating a dream, Nelly refuses to hear it: 'I was superstitious about dreams then, and am still; and Catherine had an unusual gloom in her aspect, that made me dread something from which I might shape a prophecy, and foresee a fearful catastrophe' (p. 80). After

Heathcliff's death, she dismisses as 'Idle tales' (p. 336) the stories of the country folk that Heathcliff and Catherine haunt the moors, and declares firmly 'I believe the dead are at peace' (p. 337), but despite her protestations, she is uncertain and unconvincing. She attempts to explain away her encounter with a little boy and his sheep, who refuse to go on because Heathcliff and a woman are on the path, but cannot dissipate the fear: 'He probably raised the phantoms from thinking, as he traversed the moors alone, on the nonsense he had heard his parents and companions repeat – yet still, I don't like being out in the dark, now – and I don't like being left by myself in this grim house' (p. 336).

Nelly complements Lockwood in terms of her familiarity with the protagonists and their environment, but in many ways the story she tells is as much beyond her comprehension as it is beyond Lockwood's. Barbara Schapiro suggests that 'Nelly is unable to empathize because she is unable to acknowledge or accept the instinctual, passionate life, both of her own unconscious and that of the children she mothers' (p. 42). Nelly's response to Catherine's famous declaration of love, 'I *am* Heathcliff', is impatience and incomprehension:

> She paused, and hid her face in the folds of my gown; but I jerked it forcibly away. I was out of patience with her folly!
> 'If I can make any sense of your nonsense, Miss,' I said, 'it only goes to convince me that you are ignorant of the duties you undertake in marrying; or else, that you are a wicked, unprincipled girl.' (p. 83)

Catherine's eloquent attempt to explain the complexity of her feelings is dismissed as 'folly' and 'nonsense', which Nelly treats with contempt, jerking herself away. Like Lockwood, her instinct is to retreat from and deny strong emotion. Nelly reads Catherine's torment as ignorance of 'the duties you undertake in marrying' and evidence that she is 'a wicked, unprincipled girl', and attempts to impose ideals of feminine decorum and modesty, reminding Catherine that for a woman principles and duty should come before love and passion. Similarly, during Catherine and Heathcliff's climactic final meeting, Nelly remains critical and detached: 'The two, to a cool spectator, made a strange and fearful picture. Well might Catherine deem that Heaven would be a land of exile to her, unless, with her mortal body, she cast away her mortal character also' (p. 160).

Nelly is throughout a 'cool spectator', refusing to engage or sympathize with the emotions displayed by the protagonists. She is biased and judgmental, and while much shrewder than Lockwood, demonstrates a tendency to conceal and portray herself to others in the best light, that may render her suspect. The reader must wonder why Brontë deliberately constructed the narrative in such a way that the story is filtered through the two characters who seem least able to understand or empathize with it – two 'unreliable' narrators. An analysis of the characters of Nelly and Lockwood suggests we must look carefully at all the evidence they provide about other characters – and themselves – and fill in the gaps where their comprehension is at fault. The burden of interpretation lies firmly with the reader.

CHAPTER 2

THE FIRST GENERATION

In spite of Brontë's evident interest in issues of origins and heritage, very little critical attention has been paid to the older generation of characters. Yet an analysis of the first generation of Earnshaws and Lintons sheds light on their descendants' education, prejudices, social and psychological development and attitude to power. In Mr Earnshaw, Mr Linton and Joseph, Brontë depicts the worst excesses of patriarchy, authoritarianism and religious tyranny.

MR AND MRS EARNSHAW

The Earnshaws seem rooted in their environment, particularly in their house, Wuthering Heights, which was built in 1500 by an earlier Hareton. The reader is well aware of the turbulence associated with the Heights under the drunken Hindley and demonic Heathcliff, but the house reflects a much more ancient violence. The exterior forms a defensive structure against the elements: 'Happily, the architect had foresight to build it strong: the narrow windows are deeply set in the wall, and the corners defended with large jutting stones' (p. 4). But its role is not purely pragmatic; there is: 'a quantity of grotesque carving lavished over the front, and especially about the principal door [. . .] a wilderness of crumbling griffins, and shameless little boys' (p. 4). The Gothic ornamentation of their stronghold suggests that even three centuries before Lockwood's arrival, the Earnshaws were not models of Lockwood's ideal 'homely northern farmer with a stubborn countenance, and stalwart limbs set out to advantage in breeches and gaiters' (p. 5). This is confirmed by the interior. The vast oak dresser heaving with food is undecorated, 'its entire anatomy lay bare to an inquiring eye', the floor is of 'smooth, white stone', and the chairs are 'high-backed, primitive structures, painted green' (p. 5), but they share the space with 'sundry villainous old guns, and a couple of horse-pistols, and, by way of ornament, three gaudily painted canisters' (p. 5). The plain, practical aspects of the house are complicated by ornamental objects and 'villainous' weapons, suggesting a less simple interior life for the Earnshaws.

Mr Earnshaw is similarly a mixture of the homely and the violent. Nelly says 'he had a kind heart, though he was rather severe, sometimes' (p. 36). It is his kindness that brings Heathcliff to the Heights; seeing the child starving on the streets of Liverpool, he cannot bear to leave him, and daring the wrath of his wife carries him home, 'half dead with fatigue' (p. 37). So kind is this action that several critics have argued that Mr Earnshaw must have an ulterior motive; for instance, Q. D. Leavis suggests that Heathcliff was Earnshaw's illegitimate son (p. 26), making his love for Catherine incestuous. There is no direct evidence for this in the text, but the theory is attractive because incestuous love was a common feature of Romantic poetry and Gothic novels. Mr Earnshaw suggests a much more practical explanation: 'his money and time, being both limited, he thought it better to take it home with him, at once, than run into vain expenses there' (p. 37). The Earnshaws are a respectable family, but money seems to be in fairly short supply; Mr Earnshaw walks the 120 miles to Liverpool and back rather than riding, presumably because all the horses are needed for the harvest, and Mrs Earnshaw's chief complaint is that bringing up Heathcliff will cost money 'when they had their own bairns [children] to feed, and fend for' (p. 37). The Earnshaws are nowhere near as financially secure as their neighbours, the Lintons.

Mrs Earnshaw is not drawn in great detail, and seems to have little impact on her children; she dies two years after Heathcliff's arrival, and does not seem to be mourned by her children to any extent. She takes an instant dislike to 'that gypsy brat' Heathcliff, and is 'ready to fling it out of doors' immediately (p. 37); she has previously lost a son called Heathcliff, but her maternal feelings are clearly not awakened by the interloper. The persecution of Heathcliff by Hindley and Nelly is able to continue because Mrs Earnshaw turns a blind eye: 'the mistress never put in a word on his behalf, when she saw him wronged' (p. 38).

Whether out of Christian charity or self-interest, Mr Earnshaw has rescued Heathcliff, but his treatment of his own children is less than kind, and often cruel. He is a disciplinarian; when the eight-year-old Catherine spits at Heathcliff, Mr Earnshaw gives her 'a sound blow [. . .] to teach her cleaner manners' (p. 37), and Heathcliff warns Hindley that if his father finds out about his thrashings of Heathcliff 'you'll get them again with interest' (p. 39). Eventually, to his great regret, Mr Earnshaw becomes too feeble to discipline his children: 'He seized his stick to strike him, and shook with rage that he could not do it' (p. 41). When Catherine and Heathcliff destroy his books, Joseph laments the good old days when Mr Earnshaw would have whipped them soundly: 'Ech! th' owd man ud uh laced 'em properly – bud he's goan!' (p. 21)

Perhaps more damaging than his physical chastisement is the mental abuse he inflicts on his children. He sends Hindley away to college not to educate him, but to cast him off, making it clear he has no respect or love for his son: 'Hindley was naught, and would never thrive as where he wandered' (p. 41). He is 'strict and grave' with Catherine, reading her high spirits and mischief as wickedness, and rejecting her attempts to make it up with him: 'I cannot love thee; thou'rt worse than thy brother. Go, say thy prayers, child, and ask God's pardon. I doubt thy mother and I must rue that we ever reared thee!' (p. 43). Mr Earnshaw punishes the child by withdrawing not only his own parental approval, but that of his wife and God. Catherine is 'repulsed continually' by her father; his final words to her are: 'Why canst thou not always be a good lass, Cathy?' (p. 43). His role in his children's lives is almost wholly negative, imposing restraint, silence and guilt through violence, rejection and religious indoctrination.

Most damaging of all, he uses Heathcliff against his own children. This is not just due to his pity for the 'poor, fatherless child' (p. 38), and his anger at Hindley's persecution of him, but because Heathcliff comes to represent Mr Earnshaw's power and authority. As Earnshaw's health fails, his temper becomes even more irascible, and his concern about being supplanted by his children means that 'suspected slights of his authority nearly threw him into fits' (p. 41). His children's reactions to Heathcliff act as a trigger for Earnshaw's fears about his own fading authority:

> This was especially to be remarked if any one attempted to impose upon, or domineer over, his favourite: he was painfully jealous lest a word should be spoken amiss to him, seeming to have got into his head the notion that, because he liked Heathcliff, all hated, and longed to do him an ill-turn. (p. 41)

A slight to Heathcliff is a slight to Earnshaw, because he believes his will should be law; he cannot see that his son might resent Heathcliff for taking his place in his father's affections, choosing instead to see Hindley's persecution of Heathcliff as a challenge to his father's authority. Proof that his anger is generated less by pity for Heathcliff than anxiety about his own power can be seen in the fact that Earnshaw is even more threatened by the bond between Heathcliff and Catherine; what he 'hated most' was Catherine 'showing how her pretended insolence [. . .] had more power over Heathcliff than his kindness: how the boy would do *her* bidding in anything, and *his* only when it suited his own inclination' (p. 43). Mary Burgan argues that Brontë 'shows in Mr Earnshaw the declining patriarch's lonely obsession with power, his resentment of the inheriting children and his effort to dominate the future by putting their patrimony in doubt' (Bloom, p. 136). His paranoia has terrible consequences, not just for his children, but also his grandchildren (Hareton and Catherine) in the example he sets for Hindley and Heathcliff: 'In making a weapon of one child against the others, Earnshaw establishes a mode of fatherhood that will be repeated in the generation to follow. It is a mode of violent self-assertion' (Burgan, in Bloom, p. 136).

MR AND MRS LINTON

The Lintons' home, Thrushcross Grange, expresses a different history and different social aspirations. Thirteen-year-old Heathcliff is entranced: 'ah! It was beautiful – a splendid place carpeted with crimson, and crimson-covered chairs and tables, and a pure white ceiling bordered by gold, a shower of glass-drops hanging in silver chains from the centre, and shimmering with little soft tapers' (p. 48). Everything appears new and luxurious, with carpets instead of a stone floor, wide windows with shutters and curtains rather than narrow, deep-set casements, a chandelier rather than single candles, crimson-covered chairs rather than primitive, painted ones. The Grange has an enclosed park rather than the farmed fields at the Heights, and the Lintons travel to church in the family carriage, while the Earnshaws ride.

But the Lintons' wealth engenders a siege mentality; if Mr Earnshaw is convinced that his children are challenging his authority, Mr Linton is paranoid that thieves are constantly plotting to rob him. The property is patrolled by men and dogs, and the doors are barred. When Catherine is seized by the bulldog, the Lintons' servant jubilantly calls, 'Keep fast, Skulker, keep fast!', while Mr Linton, who hovers in the safety of the entrance asks: 'What prey, Robert?' (p. 49). Their suspicions and threats of violence remain even when they see that the 'prey' is two children; Robert surmises: 'Very like, the robbers were for putting them through the window, to open the doors to the gang, after all were asleep, that they might murder us at their ease. [. . .] you shall go to the gallows for this. Mr Linton, sir, don't lay by your gun' (pp. 49–50). Linton is outraged by the idea of an attack on his house:

> The rascals knew that yesterday was my rent day; they thought to have me cleverly. [. . .] To beard a magistrate in his strong-hold, and on the Sabbath, too! where will their insolence stop? Oh, my dear Mary, look here! Don't be afraid, it is but a boy – yet, the villain scowls so plainly in his face, would it not be a kindness to the country to hang him at once, before he shows his nature in acts, as well as features? (p. 50)

Linton's house is his 'strong-hold'; its comfort and luxury belie its role as a fortress protecting his cash. Clearly the Lintons have tenants, and the carpets and chandeliers are purchased with the proceeds of 'rent day'. A robbery would be a threat to Linton's authority, expressing 'insolence' rather than the need or desire for money. The 'insolence' is compounded not only by the fact it is the Sabbath, but in that Linton is a magistrate, a symbol of the law in the region. But despite his role as a magistrate, Linton is not inclined to be just; Heathcliff is judged by his physiognomy alone, with no evidence to suggest he planned a robbery, and Linton asserts it would be perfectly acceptable to hang him to prevent him from committing crimes in the future. The temperate, benign qualities Nelly associates with the Lintons are the velvet glove on the hand of brutal authoritarianism.

To the Lintons, Heathcliff is a 'villain', a 'gipsy', 'a little Lascar, or an American or Spanish castaway', 'A wicked boy [. . .] quite unfit for a decent house' (p. 50), and Mrs Linton allows her children to visit the Heights only on condition that they are kept away from the 'naughty swearing boy' (p. 55). Their reaction to Catherine is very different; as Heathcliff notes, 'she was a young lady and they made a distinction between her treatment and mine' (p. 51). More than this, they see potential in Catherine, and determine to develop it not just for Catherine's benefit, but their own. The Linton stock is enervated, but Catherine can 'kindl[e] a spark of spirit in the vacant blue eyes of the Lintons' (p. 51), compensating with her vivacity for their want of native energy. Once they have transformed her into a lady, she will be an acceptable wife for Edgar, and they can incorporate her into their family unit. The Lintons sanction Edgar's courtship of Catherine, and when Catherine falls ill, they take over, anxious to protect their investment. Mrs Linton vigorously asserts her rights over her future daughter-in-law: 'Old Mrs Linton paid us several visits, to be sure; and set things to rights, and scolded and ordered us all; and when Catherine was convalescent, she insisted on conveying her to Thrushcross Grange' (p. 88). But both Mrs Linton and her husband succumb to Catherine's fever and die. Just as Earnshaw attempts to exert authority by inserting Heathcliff into the Heights, destroying his family in the process, the Lintons try to enrich their bloodline by appropriating Catherine, and are themselves destroyed.

JOSEPH

Many readers regard Joseph as an irritant, not because of his constant carping on souls and damnation, but because of his dialect. This was true even for the earliest readers; when Charlotte was preparing a new edition of her sister's novel in 1850, she worried about whether Joseph needed to be translated and clarified:

> It seems to me advisable to modify the orthography of the old servant Joseph's speeches – for though – as it stands – it exactly renders the Yorkshire accent to a Yorkshire ear – yet I am sure Southerns must find it unintelligible – and thus one of the most graphic characters in the book is lost on them. (Barker 1997, p. 301)

While Charlotte is concerned that his language makes him 'unintelligible', there is no doubt in her mind that he is not only authentic but 'one of the most graphic characters in the book' rather than an incidental figure. Emily Brontë would possibly have disapproved of her sister's modification; she has Joseph mock the affected speech of the upper-class Isabella: 'Mim! mim! mim! Did iver Christian body hear owt like it? Minching un' munching! Hah can Aw tell whet ye say?' (p. 137). So-called 'Standard' English may be equally unintelligible to a Yorkshire servant, and who is to say which should take precedence?

It is worth persevering with Joseph's dialect and analysing his character, as he is a potent presence in the novel. Stevie Davies states:

> The importance of Joseph cannot be over-estimated: there is only a handful of chapters in which he fails to appear, or to merit allusion, rooting the novel in locality, tradition, idiom and belief. Joseph is not a 'minor' character, standing somewhere 'behind' the gentleman-class of the romantic protagonists [. . .]. He is a gnarled root of the novel's authenticity.

[. . .] He has always been there and he always will be, old as the hills, son of the Ancient of Days, with a mythic and timeless quality that does not conflict with his authenticity as a representative of the working class with its pride in hard graft and contempt for the affectations of gentility. (p. 149)

Joseph possesses extraordinary resilience. Already a 'surly old man' (p. 22) in Catherine Earnshaw's childhood, he seems to Lockwood 'an elderly, nay, an old man, very old, perhaps, though hale and sinewy' (p. 4). He exerts a strange power over the masters of the Heights, escaping the vengeance of those he has worked against. Through 'his knack of sermonizing and pious discourse' he gains influence over Mr Earnshaw, increasing his tendency to persecute his children: '[Joseph] was relentless in worrying him about his soul's concerns, and about ruling his children rigidly' (p. 42). Despite the fact that he has widened the divide between father and son by criticizing the 'reprobate' Hindley, Joseph retains his place at the Heights when Hindley becomes master, and when Hindley becomes tyrannical, stays on not from loyalty but 'to hector over tenants and labourers; and because it was his vocation to be where he had plenty of wickedness to reprove' (p. 66). One of his tasks under Hindley is the ruthless repression of Heathcliff, whom he thrashes 'till his arm ached' (p. 47), and Heathcliff as a child comforts himself by imagining 'flinging Joseph off the highest gable' (p. 49). Yet when Heathcliff becomes master, Joseph is neither flung from the gable nor dismissed; Heathcliff not only tolerates the old man, but turns him into a weapon against Hareton and Linton. Heathcliff sends Joseph to claim Linton from Edgar, and so zealous is the old man to do his new master's bidding that he has to be literally dragged from the room (p. 203). Joseph encourages Hareton in his brutality and his pride, delighting in Heathcliff's destruction of Hareton because he sees in it proof of Heathcliff's diabolical nature: 'He allowed that [Hareton] was ruined; that his soul was abandoned to perdition; but then, he reflected that Heathcliff must answer for it. Hareton's blood would be required at his hands; and there lay immense consolation in that thought' (p. 197).

The keystone of Joseph's character is obviously his religious bigotry. According to Nelly: 'He was, and is yet, most likely, the wearisomest, self-righteous pharisee that ever ransacked a Bible to rake the promises to himself, and fling the curses on his neighbours' (p. 42). Pharisees were Jewish priests, who during the Roman occupation became renowned for hypocrisy, demanding that the people observe the letter of the law, but breaking it themselves. In Matthew 23: 25–27, Jesus criticizes them: 'Woe unto you, scribes and Pharisees, hypocrites! for ye make clean the outside of the cup and of the platter, but within they are full of extortion and excess [. . .] for ye are like whited sepulchres, which indeed appear beautiful outward, but are within full of dead *men's* bones, and of all uncleanness'. One significant image in the novel reveals Joseph's misuse of the Bible: 'he solemnly spread his large Bible on the table, and overlaid it with dirty bank-notes from his pocket-book, the produce of the day's transactions' (p. 315). He has desecrated the holy book by making it a repository for 'dirty' money, just as he has desecrated his faith by using it to dominate those who are weaker than himself. His presence in Lockwood's dream shows that even on a short acquaintance Lockwood recognizes that Joseph's religion is an alternative route to power; Joseph's pilgrim's staff, which should be a symbol of his journey to heaven, is in fact a 'heavy-headed cudgel', and during the fight in the chapel Joseph is Lockwood's 'nearest and most ferocious assailant' (pp. 23–4).

Joseph seems to believe in the Calvinist doctrine of elective salvation; he is confident that certain individuals are chosen to be saints (most notably himself), while others are damned as sinners (most of the other characters in the novel, as far as Joseph is concerned). The storm that occurs on the night of Heathcliff's disappearance is, for Joseph, divine retribution, similar to the biblical Flood, or the fate of Sodom and Gomorrah: 'Joseph swung onto his knees, beseeching the Lord to remember the Patriarchs Noah and Lot; and, as in former times, spare the righteous, though he smote the ungodly'. He prays 'that a wide distinction might be drawn between saints like himself and sinners like his master', and when he thinks Heathcliff must be dead at the bottom of a bog-hole, he is sure it is a divine blessing: 'Thank Hivin for all! All warks togither for gooid tuh them as is chozzen, and piked aht froo' th' rubbidge!' (pp. 85–6)

But the easiest way to be damned, according to Joseph, is to be female; his misogyny is deep-rooted, and he is afraid feminine wiles will prove more powerful than his dominance by fear. Women are a threat to his authority. The arrival of Isabella makes Joseph consider leaving the Heights, because he cannot bear to take orders from a woman: 'just when Aw getten used tuh two maisters, if Aw mun hev a *mistress* set o'er my heead, it's loike time tuh be flitting' (p. 141). According to Joseph, the younger Catherine is 'a nowt, and it's noa use talking – yah'll niver mend uh yer ill ways, bud goa raight tuh t'divil, like yer mother afore ye!' (p. 15). He is easily convinced that she is a witch, capable of killing the red cow and causing Joseph's rheumatism, because he fears the power of women over men. He believes Catherine has 'witched' Hareton and stolen his soul; holding Catherine responsible for the destruction of his beloved currant trees, Joseph again threatens to leave before he too can be brought under woman's yoke: 'Yah muh bend tuh th' yoak, and ye will – *Aw'm* noan used to't [. . .] Aw'd rather arn my bite, an' my sup, wi' a hammer in th' road!' (p. 319).

According to Oscar Wilde's aspiring Victorian novelist Miss Prism in *The Importance of Being Earnest* (1895), the defining characteristic of Fiction is poetic justice: 'The good ended happily, and the bad unhappily. That is what Fiction means' (p. 318). But Joseph is never really punished for his self-righteousness, hectoring, hypocrisy and tyranny. Like his enemy Heathcliff, Joseph is an outsider, his dispossession marked by his lack of a surname (presumably, unlike Heathcliff, he has one, but we are never told what it is). While Heathcliff uses money and cunning to wrest control of the Heights and the Grange from the Earnshaws and Lintons, Joseph successfully exerts himself to gain power through bigotry, fear and his willingness to do the bidding of those he believes to be damned. Having been there from the start, Joseph ends the novel as the ultimate (living) possessor of Wuthering Heights; his success marks one of the ways in which Brontë subverts the conventional Victorian 'happy ending'.

CHAPTER 3

THE SECOND GENERATION

In the second generation, the Earnshaws and Lintons form mir-
rored pairs of siblings: an elder brother (Hindley and Edgar) and
younger sister (Catherine and Isabella), who resemble each
other closely in appearance, particularly in their eyes; Heathcliff
says that Isabella's eyes 'detestably resemble Linton's', so that he
would enjoy 'turning the blue eyes black every day or two' (p. 106),
while Isabella taunts Heathcliff after Catherine's death 'I see her in
Hindley; Hindley has exactly her eyes' (p. 182). In the normal
course of things, it would have been likely that the pairs of siblings
would have intermarried; after all there seem to be no other
romantic possibilities in the vicinity, certainly no potential marriage partners. Lockwood's comment on the 'dearth of the human
physiognomy' (p. 91) in the locality suggests that there has been so
much intermarriage that all faces look the same, while Catherine
has never met anyone handsomer or richer than Edgar: 'If there
be any, they are out of my way – I've seen none like Edgar' (p. 79).
This 'dearth' will be amplified in the third generation, when
Catherine Linton marries first one of her cousins, then the other.
The arrival of Heathcliff disrupts the pattern; Hindley is banished,
and returns married to a stranger, Isabella marries Heathcliff, and
Catherine's affections are divided between Heathcliff and Edgar.
But while Heathcliff may seem the exact antithesis to both Hindley
and Edgar, who hate him vehemently, Brontë suggests subtle parallels between the three men. She also examines the ways in which
the second generation are shaped and destroyed by patterns of
power developed by their ancestors.

HINDLEY EARNSHAW

Brontë first introduces Hindley through his sister's eyes, in the role of adult domestic tyrant. Catherine's diary, read by Lockwood, is full of anger at Hindley's treatment of her and Heathcliff shortly after Mr Earnshaw's death:

> I wish my father were back again. Hindley is a detestable substitute – his conduct to Heathcliff is atrocious [. . .]. On Sunday evenings we used to be permitted to play, if we did not make much noise; now a mere titter is sufficient to send us into corners! [. . .] Poor Heathcliff! Hindley calls him a vagabond, and won't let him sit with us, nor eat with us any more [. . .]. He has been blaming our father (how dared he?) for treating H. too liberally; and swears he will reduce him to his right place [. . .] (pp. 20–2)

Hindley may blame his father, but he imposes himself as a 'substitute', more severe and repressive than Mr Earnshaw. 'You forget you have a master here,' he tells his sister and adoptive brother: 'I'll demolish the first who puts me out of temper! I insist on perfect sobriety and silence' (p. 21). He has learned the lesson of patriarchy and avails himself of its power to 'reduce [Heathcliff] to his right place', the servants' quarters. But immediately the picture is complicated by Hindley's affection for his wife: 'Frances [. . .] seated herself on her husband's knee; and there they were, like two babies, kissing and talking nonsense by the hour' (p. 21). The patriarch who demands 'sobriety and silence' becomes a child delighting in 'nonsense'. These two facets of Hindley's character – the innocent child and the vengeful man – co-exist simultaneously, reminding the reader that there is no such thing as a straightforward character in *Wuthering Heights*.

After this glimpse of the adult Hindley, Brontë uses flashback to show us the adolescent Hindley through Nelly's eyes, waiting for his father to return from Liverpool. While the Heights is associated with the primitive, bare, plain, forthright, earthy, fiery qualities as opposed to the Grange's cultivated, luxurious novelty, Hindley already has very particular tastes. Hindley's name is suggestive; it could imply *hind*er, which is what he does to Heathcliff, or be*hind*, in his feelings of having been usurped by Heathcliff. A 'hind' is also an archaic word for 'a rustic, a boor', both of which terms Lockwood uses in describing Hindley's son, Hareton. But young Hindley is much more sophisticated than his name might suggest. When asked what he would like as a present from Liverpool, Hindley asks for a fiddle; Gilbert and Gubar suggest that Hindley's desire for the fiddle demonstrates 'a secret, soft-hearted desire for culture and an almost decadent lack of virile purpose' (p. 264). Hindley longs for the civilized, educated qualities that tend to be associated with the Grange rather than the Heights, and the 14-year-old reacts to the destruction of the fiddle not by grinning and spitting, like his sister, but by 'blubber[ing] aloud' (p. 37), just as Edgar is seen 'weeping silently' after his argument with Isabella over the puppy (p. 48).

Hindley's attraction to new-fangled notions of behaviour and fashion are intensified when he is sent from the Heights to college. Significantly, like Heathcliff, Hindley stays away for three years, and returns a changed man:

> He had grown sparer, and lost his colour, and spoke and dressed quite differently: and, on the very day of his return, he told Joseph and me we must thenceforth quarter ourselves in the back-kitchen, and leave the house for him. Indeed he would have carpeted and papered a small spare room for a parlour; but his wife expressed such pleasure at the white floor, and huge glowing fire-place, at the pewter dishes, and delf-case, and dog-kennel, and the wide space there was to move about in, where they usually sat, that he thought it unnecessary to her comfort, and so dropped the intention. (p. 46)

Hindley has mysteriously turned himself into a gentleman, just as Heathcliff will do, marking the difference in his speech and dress. While part of his motivation to drag Heathcliff down to his 'right place' is clearly revenge, Hindley genuinely seems to believe in the need for a new hierarchy at the Heights; his foster-sister Nelly is also to be banished with Joseph to the back-kitchen. Had Frances wished it, he would have created a parlour for her, with carpet and wallpaper, things unknown at the Heights before; when the newly married Isabella asks Joseph, 'Have you no place you call a parlour?' he is incredulous: ' "*Parlour*!" he echoed, sneeringly, "*parlour*! Nay, we've noa *parlours*" ' (p. 141). Hindley's new pretensions are his own, rather than his wife's; Nelly notes that 'probably, she had neither money nor name to recommend her, or he would scarcely have kept the union from his father' (p. 45), so Hindley is not attempting to recreate what Frances is used to. The ruins of his aspirations can be seen in his bedroom, described by Isabella after Hindley has descended into the abyss of drunkenness:

> There was a carpet, a good one; but the pattern was obliterated by dust; a fire-place hung with cut paper dropping to pieces; a handsome oak-bedstead with ample crimson curtains of rather expensive material, and modern make. But they had evidently experienced rough usage: the valances hung in festoons, wrenched from their rings, and the iron rod supporting them was bent in an arc, on one side, causing the drapery to trail upon the floor. The chairs were also damaged, many of them severely; and deep indentations deformed the panels of the walls. (p. 142)

Hindley's tastes are clearly different from those of his parents, who were anxious about money and whose concern with function rather than fashion can be seen elsewhere in the house; the carpet and curtains in Hindley's private space are well-made and expensive, the fireplace decorated with cut paper, everything is 'handsome', 'ample' and 'modern'. But the room has suffered both from neglect and from 'rough usage', the damaged chairs and indented walls testifying to outbursts of uncontrollable rage. The distortion of Hindley's inclinations arises from two sources: his hatred of Heathcliff, and his love for Frances.

The reasons for Hindley's persecution of Heathcliff seem obvious: Heathcliff has displaced Hindley in his father's affections. Nelly notes:

> from the very beginning, he bred bad feeling in the house, and at Mrs Earnshaw's death, which happened in less than two

years after, the young master had learnt to regard his father as an oppressor rather than a friend, and Heathcliff as a usurper of his parent's affections, and his privileges, and he grew bitter with brooding over these injuries. (p. 38)

Here Hindley's view of his father as 'an oppressor' takes precedence over his feeling that Heathcliff is 'a usurper' of his father's love. Also, opposition to his father is linked specifically to his mother's death. John T. Matthews suggests that: 'Hindley [. . .] may owe less to Heathcliff's literal usurpation than to his own Oedipal, unconscious realization that every father is first his son's oppressor' (Bloom, p. 156). The arrival of Heathcliff at the point at which the adolescent Hindley might have been beginning to act on his unconscious Oedipal urges in preparing eventually to displace his father provides Hindley with an alternative focus for resentment.

After his father's death, Hindley has triumphed, and for a time seems oblivious to Heathcliff. It is his wife's aversion that changes things: 'A few words from her, evincing a dislike to Heathcliff, were enough to rouse in him all his old hatred of the boy' (p. 46). It is only at this point that Hindley decides to push Heathcliff down into his rightful place: 'He drove him from their company to the servants, deprived him of the instructions of the curate, and insisted that he should labour out of doors instead, compelling him to do so, as hard as any other lad on the farm' (p. 46). In doing so, Hindley sets a model for Heathcliff, which he follows in treating Hindley's son Hareton in exactly the same way.

Sensible Nelly is typically unimpressed by Hindley's wife, Frances, thinking her 'half silly' (p. 45) in her hysterical reaction to the black clothing of the mourners at Mr Earnshaw's funeral. Frances's fear of death is well-founded; Nelly doesn't recognize the clear symptoms of consumption (tuberculosis) Frances demonstrates – bright eyes, shallow breath, coughing, nervousness – but Dr Kenneth does, telling Hindley: 'When she came, I felt convinced we shouldn't keep her long [. . .] you should have known better than to choose such a rush of a lass!' (p. 64). But Frances's illness does not make her ineffectual; the 'rush of a lass' has a major impact on life at the Heights. Although she has 'neither money nor name to recommend her' (p. 45), she shares Hindley's class aspirations, and it is Frances who effects Catherine's transformation from savage to lady: 'Mrs Earnshaw undertook to keep her sister-in-law in due restraint [. . .] employing art, not force – with force she would have found it impossible. [. . .] The mistress [. . .] commenced her plan of reform by trying to raise her self-respect with fine clothes and flattery' (pp. 52–3). Frances succeeds where Mr Earnshaw, Hindley and Nelly have failed. She also succeeds where Isabella and Catherine fail, in giving birth to a healthy male heir, Hareton, but, like Catherine, she dies in the effort.

Hindley is devastated by the loss of his beloved wife; Nelly comments: 'he had room in his heart only for two idols – his wife and himself – he doted on both, and adored one, and I couldn't conceive how he would bear the loss' (p. 65). His desperation has obvious parallels with the grief of Heathcliff and Edgar over Catherine. While both Heathcliff and Edgar are consoled with the thought of being reunited with Catherine – though in very different ways – Hindley has no such belief to comfort him, and tries to find relief in 'reckless dissipation' (p. 66) – drinking and gambling. When he drinks, he is mad, when he does not drink he is suicidal; either way, he is intent on his own destruction. To an extent, this is an attempt to revenge himself on yet another father figure – God; when Nelly pleads with Hindley to consider his soul, he replies: 'Not I! on the contrary, I shall have great pleasure in sending it to perdition, to punish its maker' (p. 76). It may also be a reflection of a painful biographical fact; while Brontë was writing *Wuthering Heights*, her brother Branwell, who had fallen in love with a married woman, was destroying himself with drink, watched by his helpless father and sisters. He died, the year after *Wuthering Heights* was published, at the age of 31.

Hindley's sister and foster-sister never entirely lose sight of the brother they loved as children; shortly after Hindley almost kills Hareton, Catherine asks Nelly: 'You remember him [Hindley], I dare say, when he was just such another as that chubby thing [Hareton] – nearly as young and innocent' (p. 80). Later, Nelly, anxious about Hindley while Heathcliff is lodging at the Heights, finds her childhood memories revived at the sand-pillar:

I cannot say why, but all at once, a gush of child's sensations flowed into my heart. Hindley and I held it a favourite spot twenty years before.

I gazed long at the weather-worn block; and, stooping down, perceived a hole near the bottom still full of snail-shells and pebbles which we were fond of storing there with more perishable things – and, as fresh as reality, it appeared that I beheld my early playmate seated on the withered turf; his dark, square head bent forward, and his little hand scooping out the earth with a piece of slate.

'Poor Hindley!' I exclaimed, involuntarily. (p. 108)

The apparition Nelly sees is most likely Hareton (whom she sees again shortly afterwards at the Heights) rather than a spectral Hindley, but it affords a glimpse of the infant who has grown into a domestic tyrant. The reader is continually reminded that Hindley's character could have been very different had circumstances been altered.

Hindley abdicates his role as father to Hareton, who is justly terrified of him; every time Hareton encounters his father he is in danger 'of being squeezed and kissed to death [or] of being flung into the fire, or dashed against the wall' (p. 74), and on one occasion Hindley almost kills Hareton by dropping him over the banister. It is no wonder that Hareton calls him 'Devil daddy' (p. 109), and chooses an alternative father in Heathcliff. Hindley finds that the Oedipal struggle has been reversed; whereas before he had been usurped in his father's affections by Heathcliff, now he has been usurped in his son's. He also fails in his role as protector of patriarchy; Wuthering Heights should pass in an unbroken line from the Hareton Earnshaw of 1500 to the Hareton Earnshaw of the late eighteenth century, but due to Hindley's gambling debts it falls instead to Heathcliff. Hindley's final days are dominated with the loss of the Heights, the wrong done to Hareton, and his desire to revenge himself on Heathcliff: 'Am I to lose *all*, without a chance of retrieval? Is Hareton to be a beggar? Oh, damnation! I *will* have it back; and I'll have *his* gold too; and then his blood; and hell shall have his soul!' (p. 140) Ignoring Isabella's warning that 'treachery, and violence, are spears pointed at both ends – they wound those who resort to them, worse than their enemies' (p. 176), Hindley attempts to kill Heathcliff with an old pistol that has a knife attached to the barrel, and that is exactly what happens; the knife springs back, badly injuring Hindley, who falls senseless, and Heathcliff tramples his unconscious body.

Six months later, Hindley is dead, at the age of 27, and in spite of Nelly's suspicions of foul play, his death is self-inflicted; Dr Kenneth says 'He died true to his character, drunk as a lord' (p. 186). According to Heathcliff: 'that fool's body should be buried at the cross-roads, without ceremony of any kind – I happened to leave him ten minutes, yesterday afternoon; and in that interval, he fastened the two doors of the house against me, and he has spent the night in drinking himself to death deliberately!' (p. 187). But Heathcliff's suggestion that Hindley's death is a scandal – suicides being forbidden to be buried in consecrated ground – belies the fact that he is only one of a number of characters in the novel to effectively will their own death, because living without love is too painful.

EDGAR LINTON

Edgar is established from the outset as the direct antithesis to Heathcliff. Nelly says: 'The contrast resembled what you see in exchanging a bleak, hilly, coal country for a beautiful fertile valley' (p. 70). While the natural imagery in Nelly's metaphor works in Edgar's favour, Catherine uses similar similes to compare the two men with a very different result; she describes her love for Edgar as 'like the foliage in the woods', short-lived and changeable, while her love for Heathcliff 'resembles the eternal rocks beneath' (p. 82). Edgar is first introduced through Heathcliff's point of view, in his description of the illicit trip to Thrushcross Grange:

> Edgar stood on the hearth weeping silently, and in the middle of the table sat a little dog, shaking its paw and yelping, which, from their mutual accusations, we understood they had nearly pulled in two between them. The idiots! That was their

pleasure! to quarrel who should hold a heap of warm hair, and each begin to cry because both, after struggling to get it, refused to take it. We laughed outright at the petted things, we did despise them! When would you catch me wishing to have what Catherine wanted? or find us by ourselves, seeking entertainment in yelling, and sobbing, and rolling on the ground, divided by the whole room? I'd not exchange, for a thousand lives, my condition here, for Edgar Linton's at Thrushcross Grange – not if I might have the privilege of flinging Joseph off the highest gable, and painting the house-front with Hindley's blood! (pp. 48–9)

Fifteen-year-old Edgar does not emerge well from this depiction, and Heathcliff shows complete contempt for his selfish and childish behaviour. However, it is not long before Heathcliff begins to envy Edgar, and want to exchange his condition for Edgar's. While he is united with Catherine in despising 'the petted things', he has no reason to fear, but once Catherine is transformed into a lady, Heathcliff realizes the danger of his situation: 'I wish I had light hair and a fair skin, and was dressed, and behaved as well, and had a chance of being as rich as he will be!' (p. 57).

Given the belief in physiognomy demonstrated by many of the characters, Edgar's physical characteristics are significant; his light hair, blue eyes, fair skin and good manners conform to expectations of the hero of a conventional romance. Heathcliff, by contrast, with his dark hair, eyes and skin, sullen expression and gruff manner of talking and acting, seems suited to the role of villain. Indeed, Joy Ellis McLemore argues that Edgar 'is angelic beside Heathcliff and certainly comes closer than anyone else in the novel to being heroic' (p. 22). Lockwood sees much to admire in Edgar's portrait at Thrushcross Grange:

I discerned a soft-featured face, exceedingly resembling the young lady at the Heights, but more pensive and amiable in expression. It formed a sweet picture. The long light hair curled slightly on the temples; the eyes were large and serious; the figure almost too graceful. I did not marvel how Catherine Earnshaw could forget her first friend for such an individual.

> I marvelled much how he, with a mind to correspond with his person, could fancy my idea of Catherine Earnshaw. (p. 67)

Lockwood suggests Edgar was far too good for Catherine, but Edgar's physiognomy suggests he is no fit mate for fiery Catherine, not just in being 'pensive and amiable', but in his lack of masculine vigour. His face is 'soft-featured', remarkably similar to his daughter's, and his figure 'almost too graceful', too feminine for a man. Nelly confirms that Edgar 'wanted spirit in general' (p. 67), and he is characterized throughout by a lack of physical courage that casts doubt on his status as potential hero. Nelly comforts Heathcliff by pointing out: 'Edgar Linton shall look quite a doll beside you [. . .] You are younger, and yet, I'll be bound, you are taller and twice as broad across the shoulders – you could knock him down in a twinkling; don't you feel that you could?' (p. 57). Edgar 'seldom mustered courage to visit Wuthering Heights openly' during his courtship of Catherine, being terrified of Hindley, in spite of the latter's attempts to treat him civilly (p. 67). Following the reappearance of Heathcliff, Edgar reacts in a peevish and unmanly way; Catherine tells Nelly: 'He always contrives to be sick at the least cross! I gave a few sentences of commendation to Heathcliff, and he, either for a headache or a pang of envy, began to cry: so I got up and left him' (p. 98). In these scenes, Edgar appears not just pensive and gentle, but effeminate, insecure, envious, even cowardly.

However, it would be a mistake to dismiss Edgar as entirely passive and powerless:

> many readers have been misled by his almost stylised angelic qualities to suppose that the rougher, darker Heathcliff incarnates masculinity in contrast to Linton's effeminacy. [. . .] Edgar does not need a strong, conventionally masculine body, because his mastery is contained in books, wills, testaments, languages, all the paraphernalia by which patriarchal culture is transmitted from one generation to the next. (Gilbert and Gubar, pp. 280–1)

Edgar may seem an unlikely representative of 'patriarchal culture', but Brontë suggests in several scenes that this supposedly effeminate, gentle creature has access to a power that is not available to the female characters he at times resembles. A magistrate like his father before him, he embodies certain attitudes towards both the female members of his family and the 'lower orders' that mark him out as a force for the retention of conventional standards upholding patriarchy.

Nelly tends to see Edgar as a victim in his relationship with Catherine. During their courtship, she considers him to be falling into a trap: 'Ah, I thought, there will be no saving him – He's doomed, and flies to his fate!' (p. 73). Edgar witnesses Catherine in a furious temper, pinching and slapping Nelly, shaking Hareton, and finally boxing Edgar's ears. Yet the simile used to describe him at this point – wondering whether he should leave forever or propose – is strikingly ambivalent: 'The soft thing looked askance through the window – he possessed the power to depart, as much as a cat possesses the power to leave a mouse half killed, or a bird half eaten' (pp. 72–3). It is Edgar, rather than Catherine, who is figured as the predator here, suggesting the balance of power does not lie where Nelly assumes it does. Nelly's description of the 'deep and growing happiness' of the young married couple is also undermined by the metaphors she uses: 'It was not the thorn bending to the honeysuckles, but the honeysuckles embracing the thorn'; 'the gunpowder lay as harmless as sand, because no fire came near to explode it' (p. 92). In Nelly's view, the honeysuckles (Edgar and Isabella) generously 'yielded' to the thorn (Catherine), which selfishly 'stood erect' (p. 92); but the honeysuckles do not actually yield to the thorn, they embrace and enclose it, suggesting restraint, suffocation, and control, while the supposed happiness of Edgar and Catherine's marriage is built on a foundation of gunpowder. Edgar maintains peace by carefully policing his wife's emotions, secretly quashing the insubordination of servants with a 'frown of displeasure'; Nelly says he 'many a time, spoke sternly to me about my pertness; and averred that the stab of a knife could not inflict a worse pang than he suffered at seeing his lady vexed' (p. 92). Catherine frequently suffers from 'depression of spirits', which Edgar responds to with 'sympathizing silence', patiently waiting until the 'return of sunshine' (pp. 92–3). This suggests less 'deep and growing happiness' than watchful monitoring and reluctance to engage openly with Catherine's bouts of deep unhappiness, which Edgar chooses to ascribe to illness rather than dissatisfaction with their marriage.

When the fire comes in the shape of Heathcliff, it is not Catherine who explodes, but Edgar. Nelly notes:

> It ended. Well, we *must* be for ourselves in the long run; the mild and generous are only more justly selfish than the domineering – and it ended when circumstances caused each to feel that the one's interest was not the chief consideration in the other's thoughts. (p. 93)

This statement reveals Edgar is not the self-sacrificing 'example of constancy and tenderness' described by Charlotte Brontë in her 1850 Preface (p. lii); Edgar's form of selfishness may appear more acceptable to Nelly, but he is determined that his 'interest' must prevail 'in the long run'. He attempts to use his dominant class position to neutralize the threat posed by Heathcliff. Like Hindley, he tries to push Heathcliff back down to his 'right place', referring to him as 'the gipsy – the plough-boy' (p. 95), and objecting to his presence in the parlour rather than the more suitable kitchen. He also tries to shame Catherine into class-consciousness: 'Catherine, try to be glad, without being absurd! The whole household need not witness the sight of your welcoming a runaway servant as a brother' (p. 96). When Heathcliff's transformation into a gentleman deprives Edgar of his class superiority, he is 'at a loss how to address the plough-boy, as he had called him', and is forced to accept him as a guest (p. 96). Edgar struggles to preserve the façade of cold social discourse in the face of Catherine and Heathcliff's elation. Heathcliff is forthright in revealing not only his original plan to 'settle my score with Hindley; and then prevent the law by doing execution on myself' (p. 97), but also that his feelings for Catherine, now another man's wife, are unchanged. Edgar, 'striving to preserve his original tone, and a due measure of politeness', responds with the almost comically inappropriate: 'Catherine, unless we are to have cold tea, please to come to the table' (p. 97).

Unable to exert his authority over his wife without causing a breach between them, Edgar's attention is turned to his sister. Edgar is appalled to find that Isabella is in love with Heathcliff:

> Leaving aside the degradation of an alliance with a nameless man, and the possible fact that his property, in default of heirs male, might pass into such a one's power, he had sense to comprehend Heathcliff's disposition – to know that, though his exterior was altered, his mind was unchangeable, and unchanged. And he dreaded that mind; it revolted him; he shrank forebodingly from the idea of committing Isabella to its keeping. (p. 101)

While the former two issues – the degrading alliance and fears for the property – are dismissed as less important than Isabella's well-being, they are clearly significant factors in Edgar's abhorrence of the match. Edgar has very little knowledge of Heathcliff's disposition, having met him infrequently during their adolescence; his one experience of Heathcliff's violence then was having a tureen of apple sauce thrown over him for having insulted Heathcliff (p. 59). His dread, revulsion and foreboding seem disproportionate, suggesting unconscious fears of losing not just his sister but his wife to Heathcliff. Lyn Pykett has described Edgar as 'the benevolent face of patriarchy' (p. 117), but even the partial Nelly admits his treatment of Isabella is cold and merciless. While Nelly asserts that Edgar 'loves her tenderly', Isabella's defiance of his authority in her elopement with Heathcliff divides her from her brother entirely; he refuses to take any further interest in his sister, or any responsibility for the separation, arguing that 'she has disowned me' (p. 133). Her apology and entreaty for reconciliation are ignored, and while Isabella loyally defends Edgar, Heathcliff is able to taunt her with Edgar's neglect: 'your brother is wondrous fond of you too, isn't he? [. . .] He turns you adrift on the world with surprising alacrity' (p. 148).

When pushed too far, Edgar shows surprising steeliness. When he first challenges Heathcliff, demanding he leave his house, he musters all the power patriarchy provides him with. The formality of his language is striking:

'I have been so far forbearing with you, sir,' he said, quietly; 'not that I was ignorant of your miserable, degraded character, but, I felt you were only partly responsible for that; and Catherine, wishing to keep up your acquaintance, I acquiesced – foolishly. Your presence is a moral poison that would contaminate the most virtuous – for that cause, and to prevent worse consequences, I shall deny you, hereafter, admission into this house, and give notice, now, that I require your instant departure. Three minutes' delay will render it involuntary and ignominious.' (p. 114)

Nelly has already told Lockwood that Edgar 'pronounced his words as you do, that's less gruff than we talk here, and softer' (p. 70); he has the voice of an outsider, despite the fact that he has spent his entire life at Thrushcross Grange. This quiet, soft, educated, cultivated voice attempts to browbeat the 'plough-boy' with polysyllabic, legalistic language – 'acquaintance', 'acquiesced', 'contaminate', 'consequences', 'admission', 'involuntary', 'ignominious'. This contrasts with the language Edgar uses to Catherine: 'How is this? [. . .] what notion of propriety must you have to remain here, after the language which has been held to you by that blackguard? I suppose, because it is his ordinary talk, you think nothing of it – you are habituated to his baseness, and, perhaps, imagine I can get used to it too!' (p. 113). The rhythm of the sentences is entirely different – with his wife, Edgar unleashes his anger in interrogatives and exclamations, with his enemy he is ponderous and condescending.

Heathcliff mocks his effort to dominate through language: 'Cathy, this lamb of yours threatens like a bull!' (p. 114). But Edgar has another weapon; he does not need physical strength of his own when he can commandeer that of others. He has summoned 'two men out of the hall' (p. 113) to do the dirty work of actually throwing Heathcliff out if his words fail. When Catherine locks the door and Edgar is left on his own, it seems he will revert to type:

Mr Edgar was taken with a nervous trembling, and his countenance grew deadly pale. For his life he could not avert that access of emotion – mingled anguish and humiliation over-came him completely. He leant on the back of a chair, and covered his face. (p. 115)

Heathcliff asks: 'Is he weeping, or is he going to faint for fear?' (p. 115). Yet Edgar prevails; striking Heathcliff a blow to the throat 'that would have levelled a slighter man', he coolly walks out the back door, leaving Heathcliff choking with fury. He returns not to argue with or be reconciled to Catherine, but to demand an answer: 'It is impossible for you to be *my* friend, and *his* at the same time, and I absolutely *require* to know which you choose' (p. 117). Gentle Edgar has effectively asserted his rights as householder and husband against fiery Catherine and savage Heathcliff.

His success is short-lived. Initially he retreats to the symbols of his power, his books, maintaining a façade of indifference, but Catherine's illness emasculates him once more: 'No mother could have nursed an only child more devotedly than Edgar tended her' (p. 134). While his mourning for Catherine is less ostentatious than that of Heathcliff and Hindley, it is deep, and in some ways strikingly similar to Heathcliff's; when he is dying, Edgar remembers 'lying, through the long June evenings, on the green mound of [Catherine's] grave, and wishing, yearning for the time when I might lie beneath it' (p. 257). Shortly afterwards, Heathcliff describes actually opening that grave to see Catherine's body, and dreaming 'I was sleeping the last sleep, by that sleeper, with my heart stopped, and my cheek frozen against hers' (p. 289). Through 20 long years, the trajectory of both men is towards death and reunion with Catherine.

Edgar's fear of meeting Heathcliff leads him to relinquish two more patriarchal pursuits, religion and the law: he stops going to church, and ceases to be a magistrate. While Edgar's power lies in 'books, wills, testaments, leases, titles, rent-rolls, documents, languages, all the paraphernalia by which patriarchal culture is transmitted from one generation to the next' (Gilbert and Gubar, p. 281), in the end this does not help him. He fails in his efforts to be an effective father figure to the third generation of children. When Catherine and Hindley are dead,

Edgar should be Hareton's legal guardian and executor of Wuthering Heights, but he can do nothing to prevent Heathcliff taking both child and house. When Isabella dies, Edgar hopes to become a father to Linton, and 'grieved bitterly at the prospect of yielding him up, and searched in his heart how it might be avoided' (p. 202), but he has no power to prevent Heathcliff from taking Linton. Finally, Edgar cannot even protect his own daughter. Edgar 'took her education entirely on himself' (p. 189), but leaves Catherine in almost total ignorance of her history, exposing her to danger. The obvious threat is Heathcliff, who imprisons and coerces Catherine into marriage with Linton; but Catherine is also subject to that very paraphernalia of patriarchy which is supposed to be her father's mastery. Catherine has been disinherited by her grandfather's will, which leaves the property to the son of his own daughter (Linton), rather than the daughter of his son – the male line is preferred. Edgar tries desperately to wrest something back for Catherine, attempting to amend his will, but Heathcliff has bribed the lawyer to remain away until Edgar is dead. Rather than mastering patriarchal culture, Edgar is eventually mastered by it.

ISABELLA LINTON HEATHCLIFF

Isabella is the epitome of the spoiled only daughter of a wealthy family. The 11-year-old Isabella, fighting with her brother over a puppy, 'lay screaming at the farther end of the room, shrieking as if witches were running red hot needles into her' (p. 48), inspiring the contempt of the watching Heathcliff and Catherine. She shares her parents' rigid view of gipsies, crime and punishment, saying of Heathcliff: 'Frightful thing! Put him in the cellar, papa. He's exactly like the son of the fortune-teller, that stole my tame pheasant' (p. 50). Just as Edgar is a contrast to Heathcliff, Isabella is initially a foil to Catherine in behaviour and appearance. Hindley and Frances encourage Catherine's transformation by flattering her into rivalry with Isabella: 'Isabella Linton is not to be compared with her, is she [. . .]? Isabella has not her natural advantages' (p. 53). She will always be in Catherine's shadow.

Seven years later, Isabella's character has not developed much beyond this. At 18, she is 'infantile in manners, though possessed of keen wit, keen feelings, and a keen temper too' (p. 101). She is also an incurable romantic, convinced that Heathcliff's fidelity to Catherine even after her marriage to Edgar is a sign of nobility: 'Mr Heathcliff is not a fiend; he has an honourable soul, and a true one, or how could he remember her?' (p. 103). After their marriage, Heathcliff mocks Isabella's romantic fantasies; she had left home:

> under a delusion [. . .] picturing in me a hero of romance, and expecting unlimited indulgences from my chivalrous devotion. I can hardly regard her in the light of a rational creature, so obstinately has she persisted in forming a fabulous notion of my character, and acting on the false impressions she cherished. (p. 149)

By demonstrating through Isabella's experience that Heathcliff's love for Catherine does not make him good, Brontë provides a warning for those readers inclined to see Heathcliff as a 'hero of romance', more sinned against than sinning.

Worst of all, Isabella's desire for Heathcliff is spontaneous and one-sided. Edgar assumes that Heathcliff must have seduced his sister, because he cannot imagine that Isabella could breach the rules of feminine decorum by being the first to desire. Remember the reaction of the young woman Lockwood had flirted with at the sea-coast; when she returns his glances and is rebuffed, she is ashamed: 'the poor innocent [. . .] overwhelmed with confusion at her supposed mistake, persuaded her mamma to decamp' (p. 6). Women were expected to be passive and responsive rather than active and initiatory in love, waiting to be approached and either accepting or rejecting the advances of men who wished to marry them. Not so Isabella; she declares her love outright, complaining that her sister-in-law is in the way: 'You are a dog in the manger, Cathy, and desire no one to be loved but yourself! [. . .] I love him more than ever you loved Edgar; and he might love me if you would let him!' (p. 102). Her passion dissolves her ladylike exterior; it is notable that from this point many of the images associated with Isabella are bestial: Catherine describes her as 'an impertinent little monkey' (p. 102), 'tigress', and 'vixen' (p. 106), while Heathcliff stares at her 'as one might do at a strange repulsive animal, a centipede from the Indies, for instance, which curiosity leads one to examine in spite of the aversion it raises' (p. 106). Heathcliff suggests that her attraction to him is less the professed admiration of his 'honourable soul' than a most unladylike relish for the violence he is capable of:

> The first thing she saw me do, on coming out of the Grange, was to hang up her little dog, and when she pleaded for it, the first words I uttered were a wish that I had the hanging of every being belonging to her, except one: possibly, she took that exception for herself – But no brutality disgusted her – I suppose she has an innate admiration of it, if only her precious person were secure from injury! (p. 150)

The hanging dog is reminiscent of the little dog injured by Isabella and Edgar in their childhood struggle for precedence; Isabella sanctions violence against 'every being belonging to her' in the hope that she herself will be safe. Perhaps her appreciation for brutality is also linked to the safety the 'cowardly children' Edgar and Isabella felt under the protection afforded by their father, courtesy of servants, weapons and dogs. But Heathcliff's description of their relationship also suggests that of sadist and masochist:

> I never, in all my life, met with such an abject thing as she is – She even disgraces the name of Linton; and I've sometimes relented, from pure lack of invention, in my experiments on what she could endure, and still creep shamefully cringing back! (p. 150)

The horror of the sadomasochistic relationship Isabella is locked into is revealed in her statement to Nelly: 'I just hope, I pray that he may forget his diabolical prudence, and kill me! The single pleasure I can imagine is to die, or to see him dead!' (p. 151).

Isabella's social persona is gradually eroded during her stay at the Heights. Initially aloof – Joseph says 'we wer a'most too mucky tuh sow t' corn fur makking her breead' (p. 209) – she quickly realizes that she no longer has access to the comforts of Thrushcross Grange, such as a parlour or a maid-servant, and decides she must adapt in order to survive: 'I'm not going to act the lady among you, for fear I should starve' (p. 140). Her decision not to 'act the lady' is an admission of how artificial social behaviour is; desperation brings out the true character. Nelly is struck by the change in Isabella's appearance:

> Her pretty face was wan and listless; her hair uncurled; some locks hanging lankly down, and some carelessly twisted round her head. Probably she had not touched her dress since yester evening. [. . .] So much had circumstances altered their positions, that [Heathcliff] would certainly have struck a stranger as a born and bred gentleman, and his wife as a thorough little slattern! (p. 146)

Her social persona as the charming young lady had been entirely dependent on the resources of Thrushcross Grange. The veneer of gentility is superficial, and quickly wears off.

Isabella is transformed from someone who worships the masculine potential for violence of Heathcliff to someone who longs to be able to inflict violence herself. Shortly after her marriage, Hindley warns Isabella of his plan to kill Heathcliff, perhaps in the hope that she will prevent him; Hindley says 'it is some devil that urges me to thwart my own schemes by killing him' (p. 140) – he cannot kill Heathcliff until he has won back the money he has lost in gambling. But Isabella's reaction surprises Hindley:

> I surveyed the weapon inquisitively; a hideous notion struck me. How powerful I should be possessing such an instrument! I took it from his hand, and touched the blade. He looked astonished at the expression my face assumed during a brief second. It was not horror, it was covetousness. (p. 140)

The phallic 'instrument', both pistol and knife, inspires envy in Isabella, because it represents the power that has so effectively subjugated her. Her passion for Heathcliff has drawn her into a trap from which she cannot free herself, because as a wife she is entirely under his control. Isabella claims she has tried to leave him: 'I've made the attempt, but I dare not repeat it!' (p. 151). Legally, a wife could not gain a separation, and could be compelled to return to a husband, unless he could be proven (at great expense) to have been extremely cruel, and Heathcliff asserts: 'I keep strictly within the limits of the law – I have avoided, up to this period, giving her the slightest right to claim a separation' (p. 150). Heathcliff also taunts Isabella with the husband's power to judge his wife's mental fitness, and confine her, should she prove troublesome: 'No, you're not fit to be your own guardian, Isabella, now; and I, being your legal protector, must retain you in my custody' (p. 151). Under eighteenth-century marriage laws – indeed, well into the nineteenth century – a married woman did not exist legally in her own right. Brontë is exploring, through Isabella, the vulnerable position of the unhappily married woman, who has no access to money or legal protection, whose body – and the children it produces – are the property of her husband.

Isabella's eventual escape is linked to her growing sense of power. Catherine's death has devastated Heathcliff, and Isabella is able to play on his momentary weakness: 'I experienced pleasure in being able to exasperate him: the sense of pleasure woke my instinct of self-preservation' (p. 174). Whereas before she longed to be killed by Heathcliff, now she wants to survive and witness his suffering. Hindley believes that Isabella must still be in love with Heathcliff, because she prevents him from killing Heathcliff by warning him of his plot and there may be an element of truth in this, despite her protests: 'I can recollect yet how I loved him; and can dimly imagine that I could still be loving him, if – No, no!' (p. 174). But Isabella is adamant that her true motive is revenge:

> what misery laid on Heathcliff could content me, unless I have a hand in it? I'd rather he suffered *less*, if I might cause his sufferings, and he might *know* that I was the cause. Oh, I owe him so much. On only one condition can I hope to forgive him. It is, if I may take an eye for an eye, a tooth for a tooth, for

every wrench of agony, return a wrench, reduce him to my level. (p. 181)

Her desire for vengeance at all costs is strikingly similar to Heathcliff's; he too plans to reduce his enemies 'to my level', making them feel every 'wrench of agony' he has been made to experience. But Isabella has not the resources of money and masculinity available to Heathcliff, and in the end she must fail. All she can do to revenge herself is smash and burn her wedding ring, the symbol of her oppression, and flee, carrying with her the unborn child who will ultimately allow Heathcliff to triumph over the Lintons in inheriting Thrushcross Grange.

CHAPTER 4

HEATHCLIFF AND CATHERINE

At the centre of the novel is the tortured relationship between Heathcliff and Catherine Earnshaw, and it is unsurprising that readers and critics have been fascinated by the protagonists, particularly Heathcliff, at the expense of the other characters. What readers remember long after they finish the novel is the final meeting of the anguished lovers, and this is justified by the raw emotion Brontë delivers in the action and speech:

> *Why* did you despise me? *Why* did you betray your own heart, Cathy? [. . .] You loved me – then what *right* had you to leave me? What right – answer me – for the poor fancy you felt for Linton? Because misery, and degradation, and death, and nothing that God or satan could inflict would have parted us, *you*, of your own will, did it. I have not broken your heart – *you* have broken it – and in breaking it, you have broken mine. So much the worse for me, that I am strong. Do I want to live? What kind of living will it be when you – oh God! would *you* like to live with your soul in the grave? (pp. 162–3)

The desperate energy with which the lovers cling to each other – for the first and last time – in the hours before Catherine's death, and the haunting of Heathcliff through the next 20 years until his own death, demonstrate a depth of emotion rarely surpassed in literature. Brontë is intent on demonstrating the ways in which Heathcliff and Catherine have been shaped and destroyed by the society from which they emerge, just like the other characters.

But she also subverts and questions the sympathy evoked by the story of their doomed love by revealing the character traits that make them active agents in their own destruction.

HEATHCLIFF

Readers and critics can hardly be blamed for seeing Heathcliff as mysterious and enigmatic, since so many of the characters in the novel do too. Isabella asks Nelly: 'Is Heathcliff a man? If so, is he mad? And if not, is he a devil?' (p. 136). Nelly wonders: 'Is he a ghoul, or a vampire? [. . .] But where did he come from, the little dark thing, harboured by a good man to his bane?' (p. 330). Even Catherine, supposedly so close that she feels she *is* Heathcliff, fails to fully comprehend him, asking, 'What new phase of his character is this?' when Heathcliff berates her for her cruelty (p. 112). The novel is rife with speculation about his origins, motivation, actions and ultimate destination. Like the characters, many of whom seem seriously to fear that Heathcliff is a 'devil', 'ghoul' or 'vampire' rather than a mere man, many critics have hesitated to ascribe a realistic conception of character to Heathcliff. The reviewer in the *Examiner* in January 1848 complained about the inconsistency in his characterization:

> we entertain great doubts as to the truth, or rather the *vraisemblance* of the main character. The hardness, selfishness and cruelty of Heathcliff are in our opinion inconsistent with the romantic love that he is stated to have felt for Catherine Earnshaw. (Dunn, p. 286)

This suggests a very one-dimensional attitude to literary characterization on the part of the reviewer: Heathcliff loves Catherine, therefore he should be soft, selfless and gentle. As 'the main character', he ought to be attractive and heroic. Brontë's conception of character is much more sophisticated than that; as we have seen, in *Wuthering Heights* even relatively minor characters are nuanced and multi-faceted. Brontë's specific allusion to Heathcliff's 'monomania' (p. 324) emphasizes her awareness that it was possible for the psyche to be divided, and for an individual to be entirely rational and normal on most subjects while entirely insane in one particular area.

For many critics, both Heathcliff's love for Catherine and his cruelty to those he holds responsible for their separation are so melodramatic that they seem to transcend the possible. Harold Bloom suggests that Heathcliff embodies the emotional sublime, designed to inspire awe but not empathy: 'his sufferings impress us, but they scarcely move us, so little do they resemble our own' (p. 1). For Charlotte Brontë his passion is 'such as might boil and glow in the bad essence of some evil genius; a fire that might form the tormented centre – the ever-suffering soul of a magnate of the infernal world' (p. liii). He has been explained as: 'an anarchic force of nature, a mythic figure thrust into the real world, a Byronic-derived Satanic outcast, a Marxist proletarian-rebel, a representation of the Freudian Id, and a reflection of the heroine's adolescent narcissism' (Stone, in Bloom, p. 47). He has been described as a projection of Emily Brontë's suppressed rage (Powys, in Bloom, p. 13), and the incarnation of masculinity, 'the penis of Peniston [sic] Crags' (Holbrook, p. 175). But Bernard Paris disputes the view that Heathcliff should be read as a mythic or Gothic figure, or 'an archetype, symbol, or projection of the unconscious who is not supposed to be understood as though he were a person':

> Heathcliff retains his human status, however fiendlike he becomes, because Emily Brontë keeps telling us that he has been victimized and that his viciousness arises from his misery. Perhaps the strongest evidence that she meant us to see his cruelty as a natural phenomenon is the fact that several characters articulate the principle that bad treatment leads to vindictiveness and several others illustrate its operation. (pp. 241–2)

We have seen this particularly in Hindley and Isabella, who manifest an affinity for all things civil and cultured, yet are made vicious by mistreatment and disappointment. Charlotte Brontë aired her misgivings about Heathcliff publicly after her sister's death in her 1850 preface, but in August 1848, a few months before Emily's death, Charlotte wrote privately to her publisher's reader, William Smith Williams, explaining that even the demonic aspects of Heathcliff's character were understandable:

> [Heathcliff] exemplifies the effects which a life of continued injustice and hard usage may produce on a naturally perverse, vindictive, and inexorable disposition. Carefully trained and kindly treated, the black gipsy-cub might possibly have been reared into a human being, but tyranny and ignorance made of him a mere demon. (Barker 1997, p. 203)

While Charlotte highlights the societal forces moulding Heathcliff's character, implicit in her analysis is her belief that Heathcliff was not born 'human'. He is by nature 'perverse, vindictive, and inexorable', and the 'injustice' and 'hard usage' he has experienced have merely exacerbated these natural tendencies. Charlotte links this specifically to ethnic origin in the phrase 'black gipsy-cub'; the 'fierce, pitiless, wolfish man' (p. 103) has grown from a 'cub' who is identified and dehumanized specifically by race.

Yet Heathcliff's ethnic origin remains unclear. Christopher Heywood has noted that there were colonies of black slaves on Yorkshire farms in the eighteenth century, and the Brontë children set their Angrian stories in West Africa (Stoneman, p. 150), so the idea of Heathcliff as a black African, possibly an escaped slave, is not impossible. The prevalence of the belief in white racial superiority was 'one of the most shocking aspects of the Victorian sensibility' (Wilson, p. 493), so to make her protagonist a black man would have been a bold move on Brontë's part. If Heathcliff is black, in a novel set before the abolition of slavery (the slave trade in the British Empire was ended in 1807, slavery in 1833), or if he is a gipsy, an ethnic group consistently discriminated against since their arrival in Britain around the early sixteenth century, his suffering may take on wider colonial significance.

To Lockwood, Heathcliff is 'a dark-skinned gypsy in aspect, in dress and manners a gentleman' (p. 5), suggesting a distinct disparity between the terms 'dark-skinned gypsy' and 'gentleman'.

Nelly's first impression is of 'a dirty, ragged, black-haired child' speaking 'some gibberish that nobody could understand' (pp. 36–7); here he is marked out as foreign by his language rather than his physiognomy (his hair is black, but not his skin). As Terry Eagleton notes: 'It is hard to know how black he is, or rather how much of the blackness is pigmentation and how much of it grime and bile' (1995, p. 3). On his return after three years' absence, Nelly describes him as 'a tall man dressed in dark clothes, with dark face and hair', but 'the cheeks were sallow, and half covered with black whiskers' (p. 93); 'sallow' suggests yellow or light brown rather than black. To Mr Linton, he is 'that strange acquisition my late neighbour made in his journey to Liverpool – a little Lascar, or an American or Spanish castaway' (p. 50). Linton's description of Heathcliff as 'that strange acquisition' may hint at a connection to slavery, particularly given Liverpool's prominent role in the slave trade, but 'Lascar' suggests Asian, and with American and Spanish thrown in for good measure it is clear that Heathcliff's origins are not entirely evident in his physiognomy. Nelly tries to comfort Heathcliff by encouraging him to fantasize about his origins:

> You're fit for a prince in disguise. Who knows, but your father was Emperor of China, and your mother an Indian queen, each of them able to buy up, with one week's income, Wuthering Heights and Thrushcross Grange together? And you were kidnapped by wicked sailors, and brought to England. Were I in your place, I would frame high notions of my birth, and the thoughts of what I was should give me courage and dignity to support the oppressions of a little farmer! (p. 58)

Two more possible national identities – Chinese and Indian – are raised, suggesting how indeterminate Heathcliff's appearance is: the only thing that is certain is that he is not acceptably white, and if his parents are Chinese or Indian the only way he can be redeemed is if they are royal and fabulously wealthy.

Terry Eagleton and Winifred Gérin have also suggested a possible Irish origin for Heathcliff (Eagleton 1995, p. 3; Gérin, pp. 225–6); while Brontë was writing the novel, Liverpool and other ports were being flooded with refugees from the Irish famine, many of whom spoke only Irish. The novel was published in 1847, the worst year of the Great Famine, during which more than a million Irish people died of starvation and disease, and opens in 1801, the year of the Act of Union, which made Ireland part of the United Kingdom. Brontë was herself half-Irish; her father, Patrick, was born in County Down in the North of Ireland. Britain's relationship with Ireland had been troubled for many centuries; Ireland had been England's first colony, suffering waves of invasion from the twelfth century onwards and extensive settlement in the sixteenth century. The Penal Laws restricted Irish access to religion, education and land, and there was a great deal of animosity between the Irish and the English: the Irish saw the English as colonizers and usurpers, the English saw the Irish as primitive and devious. The terms 'beast', 'savage', 'lunatic' and 'demon' (applied to Heathcliff not only by the other characters, but also by the critics) are 'simply an English way of saying that he is quite possibly Irish' (Eagleton 1995, p. 3).

In the end it seems not to matter what Heathcliff's ethnic origin is; what matters is that he is the eternal 'Other', alien and outcast. In a novel obsessed with genealogy and inheritance, he stands alone: 'he is simply superfluous: he has no defined place within its biological and economic system' (Eagleton 1975, p. 106). Unlike other nineteenth-century literary orphans – Oliver in *Oliver Twist* (1837–8), Esther Summerson in *Bleak House* (1852–3), Jack Worthing in *The Importance of Being Earnest* (1895), Daniel in *Daniel Deronda* (1876) – Heathcliff is not restored to a rightful identity by finding a family and a heritage. He is uneasily slotted into the Earnshaw family, given the first name of a dead son, but deprived of the surname that would prove he belongs.

Heathcliff's literary origins are equally shady. There are clear links to Milton's Satan in *Paradise Lost* (1667), given the many references to Heathcliff as demonic, an 'imp of Satan' (p. 39), 'a most diabolical man' (p. 222), 'Lonely, like the devil, and envious like him' (p. 288). Milton's Satan is a complex and charismatic character bent on revenge against God and, like Heathcliff, he usually gets the best lines:

> Farewell happy fields
> Where joy for ever dwells: hail horrors, hail
> Infernal world, and thou profoundest hell
> Receive thy new possessor: one who brings
> A mind not to be changed by place or time.
> The mind is its own place, and in itself
> Can make a heaven of hell, a hell of heaven. (1.249–55)

Satan's defiant determination to 'make a heaven of hell, a hell of heaven' is perhaps echoed in Heathcliff's statement: 'I tell you, I have nearly attained *my* heaven; and that of others is altogether unvalued, and uncoveted by me!' (p. 333).

Byron's *Manfred* (1817) has been cited as another possible literary father for Heathcliff. Like Heathcliff, Manfred tries desperately to summon up the ghost of his dead love, but unlike Heathcliff, Manfred blames himself for the destruction of his beloved Astarte, and this terrible guilt is linked specifically to origins:

> I say 'tis blood – my blood! the pure warm stream
> Which ran in the veins of my fathers, and in ours
> When we were in our youth, and had one heart,
> And loved each other as we should not love,
> And this was shed: but still it rises up,
> Colouring the clouds, that shut me out from heaven,
> Where thou art not – and I shall never be. (2.1.24–30)

Astarte was his sister, and their incestuous love is the crime which has destroyed them both. Heathcliff and Catherine's relationship cannot be categorized as incestuous: for one thing, despite critical speculation, there is no evidence in the text that Heathcliff is Earnshaw's illegitimate son. However, Heathcliff and Catherine, inseparable as children, sharing a bed until adolescence, have been raised as if they are siblings, and if Nelly can feel as if Hindley is a 'blood-relation' on the grounds of their foster relationship, it is possible the protagonists' desire is taboo, even if it is never consummated.

There are also similarities with Byron's *The Giaour* (1813), to which Charlotte Brontë alludes in describing Heathcliff as 'a Ghoul – an Afreet' (p. liii):

> Go – and with Gouls and Afrits rave;
> Till these in horror shrink away
> From spectre more accursed than they! (ll. 784–6)

The nameless hero ('Giaour' means 'infidel', suggesting foreign, alien) falls in love with the beautiful slave Leila, who is murdered by her lord, Hassan, on discovery of the affair. The Giaour avenges her death by killing Hassan, then retreats to a monastery to die, but like Heathcliff is tormented with visions of his dead love:

> Yet, Leila! yet the form is thine!
> And art thou, dearest, chang'd so much,
> As meet my eye, yet mock my touch?
> Ah! were thy beauties e'er so cold,
> I care not – to my arms enfold
> The all they ever wish'd to hold.
> Alas! around a shadow prest,
> They shrink upon my lonely breast;
> Yet still – 'tis there – in silence stands,
> And beckons with beseeching hands! (ll. 1290–9)

Leila, like Catherine, seems to beckon her lover to join her in death, but Heathcliff achieves what the Giaour cannot; Leila has been cast into the sea, and her body lost, but Catherine has been buried and can be dug up:

> I'll tell you what I did yesterday! I got the sexton [. . .] to remove the earth off her coffin lid, and I opened it. I thought, once, I would have stayed there, when I saw her face again – it is hers yet – he had hard work to stir me; but he said it would change, if the air blew on it [. . .]. I shall be a great deal more

comfortable now; and you'll have a better chance of keeping me underground, when I get there. (pp. 288–9)

Brontë translates Byron's fairly conventional yearning for reunion after death into something much more disturbing and sensational with the concrete details about the actual corpse of the beloved, and the suggestion of necrophilia and vampirism.

A third possible source is Brontë's own early works. Although the Gondal sagas are classed as 'juvenilia', Brontë continued to produce Gondal poetry well into adulthood, including while writing *Wuthering Heights*. Juliet Barker argues that 'Many of the themes and incidents in the story can be traced back to the Brontës' juvenile writings, from the death-defying love of Heathcliff and Catherine to Heathcliff's deliberate ruin of the Earnshaw and Linton families' (1995, p. 502). Heathcliff may be a recreation of the 'dark, brooding outlaw' Douglas, in Emily and Anne's Gondal writings, whose 'sole redeeming feature' is his love for the Queen of Gondal, Augusta (Barker 1995, p. 501), or the African Quashia in the Brontës' Glasstown stories (Gérin, p. 283). Several of Emily's Gondal poems reflect the idea of a foster-brother and sister who become lovers (Ratchford, p. 240). But his literary origins cannot provide the answers missing in his genetic origins: 'Despite his lineage, Heathcliff's greatest distinction as a literary character consists in his originality' (Bloom, p. 1).

Brontë first introduces Heathcliff through the notoriously erroneous viewpoint of Mr Lockwood. Initially, Lockwood regards Heathcliff as 'A capital fellow!' (p. 3), but soon changes his mind when he hears Heathcliff speak rudely to young Catherine: 'The tone in which the words were said revealed a genuine bad nature. I no longer felt inclined to call Heathcliff a capital fellow' (p. 12). The first-time reader, still trying to decide which impression is most accurate, is further confused by the anguished emotion of Heathcliff's response to Lockwood's dream:

He got on to the bed, and wrenched open the lattice, bursting, as he pulled at it, into an uncontrollable passion of tears.

'Come in! come in!' he sobbed. 'Cathy, do come. Oh do – *once* more! Oh! my heart's darling, hear me *this* time – Catherine, at last!' (p. 28)

It is impossible not to be moved by this grief, and Heathcliff's tears and endearments suggest an individual capable of deep affection and feeling. Yet the next time we see him, he is snarling at young Catherine: ' "You shall pay me for the plague of having you eternally in my sight – do you hear, damnable jade?" [. . .] Heathcliff lifted his hand, and the speaker sprang to a safer distance, obviously acquainted with its weight' (p. 30).

Lockwood is intrigued by this ambivalent character, and pumps Nelly for information: 'He must have had some ups and downs in life to make him such a churl' (p. 35). This is of course a massive understatement; the 'ups and downs' of Heathcliff's life have been catastrophic. Apparently abandoned to starve on the streets of Liverpool, the characteristic that first defines him is hardness: Nelly describes him as 'Rough as a saw-edge, and hard as whinstone!' (p. 35), 'a sullen, patient child; hardened, perhaps, to ill-treatment', 'uncomplaining as a lamb; though hardness, not gentleness, made him give little trouble' (p. 38). His experiences prior to his arrival at the Heights have evidently been painful, and he has learnt to bear suffering without tears or complaints because there has been no one to comfort him. To Nelly, he seems ungrateful, never giving any sign of love for his rescuer: 'He was not insolent to his benefactor; he was simply insensible, though knowing perfectly the hold he had on his heart' (p. 39). Yet, on discovering Earnshaw dead, both Heathcliff and Catherine 'set up a heart-breaking cry'; later, Nelly overhears the children: 'The little souls were comforting each other with better thoughts than I could have hit on; no parson in the world ever pictured Heaven so beautifully as they did, in their innocent talk' (p. 44). The 'hardened' child may not always be capable of expressing affection, but he undoubtedly feels it.

In his relationship with Hindley, Heathcliff demonstrates his intimate childhood awareness of the way the world works. He knows that in order to achieve what he wants, he will have to suffer and manipulate others. For instance, when Heathcliff's colt falls lame, he capitalizes on his pain to get his own way:

> You must exchange horses with me; I don't like mine, and if you won't I shall tell your father of the three thrashings you've given me this week, and show him my arm, which is black to the shoulder. [. . .] you will have to, and if I speak of these blows, you'll get them again with interest. (p. 39)

Following another thrashing, Heathcliff says: 'I'm trying to settle how I shall pay Hindley back' (p. 61). It is no coincidence that the language is that of commerce – 'exchange', 'interest', 'settle', 'pay'; Heathcliff's sufferings are subtly linked to money – the 'capital fellow' must become a capital*ist* fellow, must accumulate capital, in order to revenge himself on his oppressors. V. S. Pritchett argues:

> There is a faint suggestion of the Victorian social conscience in the creation of him. He is the slum orphan. He represents, in a sense perhaps remote, the passion of the outraged poor. – So utterly crushed, he will crush utterly if he arises. He has the exorbitant will to power. (Bloom, p. 16)

His revenge on the Earnshaws and Lintons may represent Victorian anxieties about the potential of the dispossessed lower class to usurp the rights and privileges of the well-off middle and upper classes.

Heathcliff's lack of money destroys his hope of marrying Catherine; 'if Heathcliff and I married', she acknowledges, 'we should be beggars' (p. 82). His answer is to set about accumulating enough wealth to protect him from rejection again. Rick Rylance describes Heathcliff as 'a gothic version of the self-made man' (Glen, p. 166); the 'self-made' man was a pervasive idea in post-Industrial Revolution Britain, where, it was suggested, any man could work himself out of poverty and eventually become a gentleman. One of the most popular books of the Victorian period, Samuel Smiles's *Self-Help* (1859) (which had begun as a series of lectures in the 1840s), was full of aspirational examples of men who had become rich and successful through hard graft. Heathcliff challenges this model of non-threatening appropriation:

> Heathcliff has shown that upward mobility is available not only through a combination of high-minded diligence and talent but through low-mindedness, ruthlessness, and opportunism at the expense of others. [. . .] The account is a dark rewriting of Smiles's exemplary tales of upward social mobility [. . .] (Ingham, p. 127)

No one knows where Heathcliff's money comes from. Lockwood wonders did he: 'escape to America, and earn honours by drawing blood from his foster country? or make a fortune more promptly, on the English highways?' (p. 92). The first suggestion is intriguing; Susan Meyer points out that Heathcliff's absence occurs between 1780 and 1783, during the last three years of the American Revolutionary War:

> By suggesting that Heathcliff has been in the American army in the years he was away, Brontë associates him with the archetypal war of successful colonial rebellion, one in which England was even at one point in fear of invasion. (p. 115)

Lockwood's early description of his 'erect and handsome figure' (p. 5) and Nelly's comment on Heathcliff's return that 'His upright carriage suggested the idea of his having been in the army' (p. 96) add weight to the idea that Heathcliff has earned his money fighting not only for his own independence, but also for America's, offering yet another colonial possibility to the characterization of Heathcliff.

It is not enough for Heathcliff that he is now sufficiently wealthy and well-spoken to be acceptable at both the Heights and the Grange. His accumulation of money and property is only beginning, and Catherine notes with concern that: 'Avarice is growing with him a besetting sin' (p. 103). Even when he is master of both the Heights and the Grange, Heathcliff is still unsatisfied:

Rich, sir! [. . .] He has, nobody knows what money, and every
year it increases. Yes, yes, he's rich enough to live in a finer
house than this; but he's very near – close-handed [. . .] he
could not have borne to miss the chance of getting a few hun-
dreds more. It is strange people should be so greedy, when they
are alone in the world! (p. 34)

His tenants consider him a 'cruel hard landlord' (p. 197), and he
tells Lockwood, 'I never relent in exacting my due, from any one'
(p. 304). As a child he was chased from the Grange by a bulldog;
now his own dogs patrol his property, and he demonstrates the
same suspicions as Mr Linton: 'They won't meddle with persons
who touch nothing [. . .]. The dogs do right to be vigilant' (p. 7);
'A stranger is a stranger, be he rich or poor – it will not suit me to
permit any one the range of the place while I am off guard!'
(p. 16). He becomes a cruel and abusive father not only to his own
son, but to Hindley's son and Catherine's daughter. He delivers 'a
shower of terrific slaps' to young Catherine, telling her: 'I know
how to chastise children, you see [. . .]. I shall be your father to-
morrow – all the father you'll have in a few days – and you shall
have plenty of that [. . .] you shall have a daily taste, if I catch such
a devil of a temper in your eyes again!' (p. 271). Heathcliff begins
by rebelling against the forces that reject him, but ends by becoming the epitome of the authoritarian, patriarchal, capitalist
society that he hates: 'It is a misreading to see Emily Brontë's hero
as challenging the system. The adult Heathcliff does not challenge
the system; he *represents* it' (Torgerson, p. 105).

Even his love for Catherine, which tends to be regarded as
metaphysical, mystical and anti-authoritarian, is figured as a
hierarchical power struggle. Catherine is not his lover, but his
'tyrant' and 'murderer'. Heathcliff submits to Catherine's dominance, but demands the right to dominate others in return:

The tyrant grinds down his slaves and they don't turn against
him, they crush those beneath them – You are welcome to
torture me to death for your amusement, only, allow me to
amuse myself a little in the same style – And refrain from
insult, as much as you are able. (p. 112)

Heathcliff's sense of being ground down by Catherine is reflected in his attempt to control his disappointment and anger by 'crushing his nails into his palms, and grinding his teeth to subdue the maxillary convulsions' (p. 26) on finding Lockwood rather than the longed-for ghostly Catherine in the bedroom they shared as children. He has to grind down and subdue the 'moral teething' that would prevent him from achieving satisfaction in the destruction of his enemies: 'I have no pity! I have no pity! The more worms writhe, the more I yearn to crush out their entrails! It is a moral teething, and I grind with greater energy, in proportion to the increase of pain' (p. 151). His experiences have taught him to treat any weakness, in himself or others, with contempt and brutality: 'It's odd what a savage feeling I have to anything that seems afraid of me! Had I been born where laws are less strict, and tastes less dainty, I should treat myself to a slow vivisection of those two, as an evening's amusement' (p. 270).

Heathcliff may be an enigma to the other characters, but he makes no effort to hide his motivation for revenge, or the means he will take to achieve it. On his return after three years' absence, he outlines for Catherine his original intentions: 'I meditated this plan – just to have one glimpse of your face – a stare of surprise, perhaps, and pretended pleasure; afterwards settle my score with Hindley; and then prevent the law by doing execution on myself' (p. 97). He tells Isabella that she will be Edgar's proxy in suffering, and long before their imprisonment reveals to Nelly the 'whole scope' of his plan to marry young Catherine to Linton to ensure Edgar's property falls to him (p. 215). He rarely disguises his actions, and makes no apology for them. Heathcliff dies with no regrets for his cruelty to his own son, Hareton and Catherine. When Nelly suggests he should repent for his 'selfish, unchristian life' and send for a minister before he dies, Heathcliff retorts: 'I've done no injustice, and I repent of nothing' (p. 333). Given his actions, this seems ludicrous. Several critics have suggested that Heathcliff cannot be judged according to conventional moral considerations; Dorothy Van Ghent says that Heathcliff is 'no more ethically relevant than is flood or earthquake or whirlwind' (Bloom, p. 18), while Lord David Cecil argues:

He is not [. . .] a wicked man voluntarily yielding to his wicked impulses [. . .] he is a natural force which has been frustrated of its natural outlet, so that it inevitably becomes destructive; like a mountain torrent diverted from its channel, which flows out on the surrounding country, laying waste whatever may happen to lie in its way. (Bloom, p. 15)

Others suggest Brontë means us to judge Heathcliff; his cruelty is meticulously catalogued and clearly premeditated, and the narrative structure ensures that his actions are 'seen from the point of view of the tortured ones as well, and hence seen for what they are' (Inga-Stina Ewbank, in Bloom, pp. 27–8). He is no Manfred or Giaour, haunted by his sin; this is 'Byron with the glamour gone' (Ewbank, in Bloom, p. 27). But Brontë has also ensured that Heathcliff's acts of revenge are parodic reflections of wider social practice, and he is correct in saying he has 'done no injustice' in that he has stuck rigidly to the letter of the law: 'The weapons he uses against the Earnshaws and Lintons are their own weapons of money and arranged marriages. He gets power over them by the classic methods of the ruling class, expropriation and property deals' (Arnold Kettle, in Stoneman, p. 140). If he has proved himself villainous, he is not punished; whether we believe the stories of his ghostly wanderings on the moors with Catherine or not, his death is triumphant. His eyes, with their 'frightful, life-like gaze of exultation' (p. 335) disturb Nelly in declaring that he has succeeded in reaching his heaven, and has not been punished for disregarding that of others.

CATHERINE EARNSHAW LINTON

Critical attention tends to focus on Heathcliff as the most important and complex character in *Wuthering Heights*; Harold Bloom's choice of Heathcliff for his *Major Literary Characters* series suggests his dominance of the novel. But it could be argued that the central figure in the novel is not Heathcliff but Catherine; Stevie Davies asserts that the 'primary figure in the novel is Cathy, Heathcliff having the status of a shadow she casts' (p. 213). The idea that the heroine might be a more compelling and sophisticated character than the hero would not have been an alien one to Brontë; as Ingham suggests, the Byronic hero is translated by Emily into a Byronic heroine in the Gondal sagas, 'a larger-than-life queen with a name to match: Augusta Geraldine Almeda' (Ingham, p. 78). The beautiful, passionate and proud Augusta seems a prototype of Catherine, at 15 'the queen of the country-side [. . .] a haughty, headstrong creature' (p. 66). Augusta is cruel and manipulative, and casts away lovers at whim – at least one of whom later commits suicide – and she is eventually assassinated by Douglas, at the instigation of Angelica, whose lover Augusta had stolen away and destroyed. But Catherine shares neither Augusta's cruelty nor her power; caught in a love triangle, she tries desperately to maintain her loyalty to both Edgar and Heathcliff, and it is her inability to control the situation that eventually destroys her.

As a child, it is Catherine's wildness and energy that seem most characteristic of her:

> we had not a minute's security that she wouldn't be in mischief. Her spirits were always at high-water mark, her tongue always going – singing, laughing, and plaguing everybody who would not do the same. A wild, wick slip she was – but, she had the bonniest eye, and sweetest smile, and lightest foot in the parish; and, after all, I believe she meant no harm; for when once she made you cry in good earnest, it seldom happened that she would not keep you company, and oblige you to be quiet that you might comfort her. (p. 42)

It is impossible not to notice Catherine, and that is perhaps the point of her 'mischief', 'singing, laughing and plaguing'; the child craves attention, and is happy to get it any way she can: 'she was never so happy as when we were all scolding her at once, and she defying us with her bold, saucy look, and her ready words' (p. 43). Her father only praises Catherine when she is ill, and therefore much quieter than usual, suggesting what he thinks a girl should be like always, silent and still: 'Why canst thou not always be a good lass, Cathy?' (p. 43). Instead of accepting the rebuke as a dutiful daughter should, Catherine reacts by turning the question back to him: 'Why cannot you always be a good man, father?' (p. 43). Their lack of understanding is emphasized by the difference in their language: Earnshaw uses archaic, dialectal and informal terms – 'canst', 'thou', 'lass', 'Cathy' – while Catherine uses more modern and formal terms – 'cannot', 'you', 'man', 'father'. Catherine subverts her father's role as patriarchal judge by asserting that he is at fault also, and is not always either a good man, or a good father. Catherine knows that she cannot win her father's approval by being 'a good lass' without the most extreme repression of her character, so she chooses to provoke him instead, and is told repeatedly, 'I cannot love thee': 'That made her cry, at first; and then, being repulsed continually hardened her, and she laughed if I told her to say she was sorry for her faults, and beg to be forgiven' (p. 43). She can only be acceptable if she apologizes for her nature, and begs forgiveness for being herself. At the heart of a comfortable domestic home, Catherine's experience of neglect and rejection 'hardened' her, just as her second self, Heathcliff, is 'hardened' on the streets of Liverpool (p. 38).

It is often forgotten that Catherine's identification with Heathcliff does not begin immediately. Six-year-old Catherine is even more vehement in her rejection of the newly arrived Heathcliff than Hindley or Nelly; she spits at Heathcliff, and refuses to allow him into the bed she shares with Hindley. Heathcliff has been responsible for the loss of her present from Liverpool – a whip. If Hindley's broken present, a fiddle, represents his desire for culture and gentility, Catherine's desire for a whip seems even more suggestive: 'symbolically, the small Catherine's longing for a whip seems like a powerless younger daughter's yearning for power' (Gilbert and Gubar, p. 264). Catherine's desire for control frequently emerges in physical violence; as a child she 'liked, exceedingly, to act the little mistress; using her hands freely, [. . .] slapping, and ordering' (p. 42). At 15, Catherine pinches Nelly 'with a prolonged wrench, very spitefully on the arm', then delivers 'a stinging blow that filled both eyes with water' (p. 71). She shakes Hareton 'till the poor child waxed livid', and when Edgar interposes he feels her hand 'applied over his own ear in a way that could not be mistaken for jest' (p. 72). Even when she is dying, she has strength enough to seize Heathcliff by the hair so forcefully that she 'retained, in her closed fingers, a portion of the locks she had been grasping' (p. 160). In all three cases her violence is a reaction to being thwarted in her attempts to exert control: when she tries 'to act the little mistress', Nelly refuses to bear it; when she knows she may be elevated to an enviable social position as Edgar's wife, Nelly refuses to leave the room; when she knows she is dying, she wants to take Heathcliff with her: 'I wish I could hold you [. . .] till we were both dead!' (p. 160). She has no control over these outbursts, which are manifestations of rage linked to her dispossession as a daughter and a woman, but which she has been taught she must suppress in order to be 'a good lass'.

On Nelly's return from her banishment for casting Heathcliff out onto the landing, she finds that 'Miss Cathy and he were now very thick' (p. 38). Nelly's absence renders Catherine's change of heart mysterious. If Catherine's desire for a whip symbolizes her unconscious awareness of her lack of power within the family, it seems odd that she would welcome the interloper whom her father openly favours not only above Hindley, but above herself. Gilbert and Gubar suggest that Catherine's alliance with Heathcliff is a recognition that he could be an alternative route to power; Catherine 'gets her whip' in the shape of Heathcliff (p. 264). She begins to use that power almost immediately to defy her father, by demonstrating 'how the boy would do *her* bidding in anything, and *his* only when it suited his own inclination' (p. 43). While her own violent rage is continually thwarted, Catherine is aware of the potential to enact her vengeance vicariously through Heathcliff. Frequently, Heathcliff is imaged as a supernatural force kept in check or unleashed by Catherine. Catherine reassures Nelly that Hindley is safe from Heathcliff: 'I stand between him and bodily harm' (p. 100). She tells Isabella: 'I never say to him "let this or that enemy alone, because it would be ungenerous or cruel to harm them," I say "let them alone, because *I* should hate them to be wronged"' (p. 103). Heathcliff also acknowledges the control Catherine wields, when he describes his restraint in not murdering Edgar:

I wish you had sincerity enough to tell me whether Catherine would suffer greatly from his loss. The fear that she would restrains me; and there you see the distinction between our feelings – Had he been in my place, and I in his, though I hated him with a hatred that turned my life to gall, I never would have raised a hand against him. [. . .] I never would have banished him from her society, as long as she desired his. The moment her regard ceased, I would have torn his heart out, and drank his blood! But, till then – if you don't believe me, you don't know me – till then, I would have died by inches before I touched a single hair of his head! (pp. 147–8)

It is as if Catherine has summoned a ghoul or vampire from the abyss to do her bidding, holding it back from those she loves, but causing it to enact an awful vengeance the 'moment her regard ceased'. But Catherine cannot always control her whip, and Heathcliff decides to take his own revenge; he will not harm Edgar directly, but he seeks to hurt him through his proxy, Isabella. Nelly's comment, 'The spirit which served her was growing intractable: she could neither lay nor control it' (p. 113), reveals that Catherine no longer has the power to make Heathcliff 'do *her* bidding in anything' (p. 43).

Catherine's emotional investment in Heathcliff is huge, and the idea of separation from him causes her great anxiety. Nelly notes that: 'The greatest punishment we could invent for her was to keep her separate from [Heathcliff]' (p. 42). Even when she is contemplating marriage to Edgar, and a move to Thrushcross Grange, she threatens that anyone who would try to separate her from Heathcliff would 'meet the fate of Milo!' (p. 82), and his disappearance is so traumatic it almost kills her. Catherine's initial rejection of Heathcliff quickly becomes complete self-identification with him, demonstrated most famously in her assertion 'I *am* Heathcliff' (p. 82). He is entirely necessary to her existence, a double who ensures her continued survival:

I cannot express it; but surely you and every body have a notion that there is, or should be, an existence of yours beyond you. What were the use of my creation if I were entirely contained here? My great miseries in this world have been Heathcliff's miseries, and I watched and felt each from the beginning; my great thought in living is himself. If all else perished, and *he* remained, I should still continue to be; and, if all else remained, and he were annihilated, the Universe would turn to a mighty stranger. I should not seem a part of it. (p. 82)

Sigmund Freud notes that the prevalent theme of the double, or *doppelgänger*, in literature (particularly Gothic literature) is:

marked by the fact that the subject identifies himself with someone else, so that he is in doubt as to which his self is, or substitutes the extraneous self for his own. In other words, there is a doubling, dividing and interchanging of the self. (p. 356)

This tendency, Freud argues, belongs to the 'primary narcissism' shared by children and 'primitive man', and originates in fear: 'For the "double" was originally an insurance against the destruction of the ego [. . .] and probably the "immortal" soul was the first "double" of the body' (p. 356). Like Emily Brontë, Catherine has had early experience of bereavement: by the time she was 6 (the same age Catherine is when Heathcliff arrives), Brontë had lost her mother and her sisters Maria and Elizabeth; Catherine's mother dies when she is around 8, but prior to this she has lost a brother called Heathcliff. Catherine only becomes 'very thick' with the 'gipsy brat' after he has been given the name of her dead brother, as if he is a revenant from the grave, or an assurance of the possibility of survival after death. Catherine ensures the survival of her own identity by investing part of it in this new Heathcliff: 'If all else perished, and *he* remained, I should still continue to be'.

Many critics have argued that Heathcliff is necessary to Catherine to fill a lack in her psyche. Stevie Davies uses the psychologist Carl Jung's idea of the projection of the part of one's psyche that is the opposite of one's biological gender, to suggest that Heathcliff is Catherine's ' "boy-self" ' – in Jungian terms, her *animus*' (p. 213). In this sense, investment in Heathcliff is a way of cheating not just death but biology and social constraint. Others have suggested that Heathcliff represents the 'id', the primitive, instinctive part of the unconscious, Catherine the 'ego', the part of the mind in which individuality resides, while Edgar is the 'super-ego', the agency of conscience, guilt and social control (Gilbert and Gubar, p. 281; Linda Gold, in Mitchell, p. 33). Catherine's choice between Heathcliff and Edgar is therefore a choice between herself as a rebellious girl, 'half savage and hardy, and free' and a conventional woman, 'Mrs Linton, the lady of Thrushcross Grange' (p. 125).

Much attention has focused on the climactic scene in Chapter 9, when Catherine reveals to Nelly her reasons for marrying Edgar, unaware that Heathcliff is listening. Catherine has already made her choice – Nelly reminds her 'You have pledged your word, and cannot retract' (p. 78) – but wants to be convinced that she has made the right decision. Her reasons for marrying Edgar are superficially selfish: 'he will be rich, and I shall like to be the greatest woman of the neighbourhood, and I shall be proud of having such a husband' (p. 78). For a girl who has yearned all her life for control, it would be difficult to resist the temptation of becoming 'the greatest woman of the neighbourhood', escaping from 'a disorderly, comfortless home into a wealthy respectable one' (p. 79). It is often suggested that Catherine marries Edgar for entirely mercenary reasons, seduced by his wealth and the luxury of Thrushcross Grange, but Catherine stresses there are three reasons for her decision: the first is 'the satisfaction of my whims'; however, the second is 'for Edgar's sake, too, to satisfy him' (p. 82), which suggests that she does love Edgar and wants to make him happy (or that she hopes to placate her super-ego). The third and most important reason is not her own escape from her 'disorderly, comfortless home', but Heathcliff's: 'if I marry Linton, I can aid Heathcliff to rise, and place him out of my brother's power' (p. 82). Marriage to Heathcliff might satisfy the id, but not the ego and super-ego, which would identify the match as a catastrophic social failure: 'It would degrade me to marry Heathcliff, now [. . .]. [I]f Heathcliff and I married, we should be beggars' (pp. 81–2). She tries to convince herself that id, ego and super-ego can merge only in her marriage to the handsome, wealthy, eminently respectable Edgar. Yet all along she knows it is wrong; unlike Lockwood, she knows herself well enough to analyse her own dream:

> heaven did not seem to be my home; and I broke my heart with weeping to come back to earth; and the angels were so angry that they flung me out, into the middle of the heath on the top of Wuthering Heights; where I woke sobbing for joy. [. . .] I've no more business to marry Edgar Linton than I have to be in heaven [. . .] (p. 81)

But the crucial period in Catherine's life is not her fifteenth year, when she decides to marry Edgar Linton and Heathcliff disappears. The scene that keeps being replayed in the novel is her separation from Heathcliff when she is 12.

Catherine is first introduced to the reader, appropriately, as not double but triple in her identity; Lockwood reads on the ledge of the little closet in which she slept with Heathcliff as a child 'a name repeated in all kinds of characters, large and small – *Catherine Earnshaw*, here and there varied to *Catherine Heathcliff*, and then again to *Catherine Linton*' (p. 19). The three names represent potential selves, only two of which are realized in her own person – it is her daughter who is Catherine Heathcliff when Lockwood reads the names. Lockwood's terrifying dream of the spectral child is prefigured in Catherine's scratched writing: 'a glare of white letters started from the dark, as vivid as spectres – the air swarmed with Catherines' (p. 20).

Lockwood tries to cancel the 'obtrusive name' by opening her books, only to find Catherine here also, both in the inscription in her Testament, 'Catherine Earnshaw, her book' (p. 20), and in the margins, which she has commandeered for her diary. Her books are 'select' (p. 20), probably all religious texts she did not choose herself; Lockwood notes the Testament and 'Seventy Times Seven, and the First of the Seventy First', the sermon which inspires Lockwood's first nightmare. Catherine's diary, written in the margins of her religious texts, is symbolic of her marginal status, not just as 'a powerless orphan in her brother's house, with no paper on which to record her story' (Gargano, pp. 81–2), but as a woman, and, in terms of the text's chronology, a corpse who nevertheless asserts her presence through her 'obtrusive name'. She subverts the legitimate patriarchal word of religion with her own illegitimate language of rebellion: 'H. and I are going to rebel – we took our initiatory step this evening' (p. 20). If Heathcliff has signalled his independence by fighting against England in the American army, George Washington Peck notes that Catherine's announcement of their rebellion is made in the year of the Declaration of American Independence (Stoneman, p. 150).

But the 'initiatory step' of Catherine's rebellion is disastrous. The diary opens shortly after Mr Earnshaw's death. Hindley is demonstrating his power over Catherine and Heathcliff by forcing them to listen to Joseph's three-hour sermon in the freezing garret while he and Frances bask by the fire. They react by destroying the appropriately titled books: 'Miss Cathy's riven th' back off "Th' Helmet uh Salvation," un' Heathcliff's pawsed his fit intuh t' first part uh "T' Brooad Way to Destruction!" ' (p. 21). Hindley flings them into the back-kitchen, from which they escape for a 'scamper on the moors' (p. 22) under the dairy woman's cloak. This section of the diary ends here, but we can take up the scene from Heathcliff's description of events to Nelly several chapters later, because the 'initiatory step' of rebellion takes Catherine to Thrushcross Grange.

After laughing at Edgar and Isabella through the window, and making 'frightful noises to terrify them still more' (p. 49), Catherine and Heathcliff are chased as suspected robbers, and Catherine is mauled by the bulldog Skulker: 'The devil had seized her ankle [. . .] I heard his abominable snorting. [. . .] The dog was throttled off, his huge, purple tongue hanging half a foot out of his mouth, and his pendant lips streaming with bloody slaver' (p. 49). Gilbert and Gubar argue that Catherine's injury is hugely significant: the dog's 'huge, purple tongue' and 'pendant lips' are obviously phallic, bleeding has sexual connotations when associated with pubescent girls, and injuries to the feet symbolize castration, as in the stories of Oedipus, Achilles and the Fisher King: 'In a Freudian sense, then, the imagery of this brief but violent episode hints that Catherine has been simultaneously catapulted into adult female sexuality *and* castrated' (p. 272). She is forcibly removed from her 'animus', the male part of herself, which she associates with Heathcliff, and coerced into the ultra-femininity valued by patriarchal society. Catherine, sick with pain, faints, and is carried into the Grange, where she is recognized in part because of the mourning clothes she wears for her father. Mrs Linton removes 'the grey cloak of the dairy maid which we had borrowed for our excursion' (p. 51), a servant washes her feet, and the Lintons ply her with negus (a hot drink of port, sugar, lemon and spice) and cakes. Heathcliff, on the other hand, is dragged from the house: 'she was a young lady and they made a distinction between her treatment and mine' (p. 51). For the first time, Catherine is made aware that she is a 'young lady', and she begins to be groomed for her new role.

After five weeks with the Lintons, she returns transformed from a 'wild, hatless little savage' into 'a very dignified person, with brown ringlets falling from the cover of a feathered beaver, and a long cloth habit which she was obliged to hold up with both hands that she might sail in' (p. 53). She cannot pet the dogs in case they 'fawn upon her splendid garments'; she kisses Nelly 'gently' rather than 'rushing to squeeze us all breathless', because Nelly is covered in flour and 'it would not have done' (p. 53). When Hindley invites Heathcliff to 'wish Miss Catherine welcome, like the other servants', she embraces him, but gazes anxiously at his 'dusky fingers', fearful that her dress 'gained no embellishment from its contact with his' (pp. 54–5). Her new clothes impose rigid constraints which are symptomatic of a new fragmentation of her identity, in which she struggles to maintain her old relationship with Heathcliff while developing a new one with the Lintons, leading her 'to adopt a double character without exactly intending to deceive anyone' (p. 67). Her alter-ego, Heathcliff, by contrast, diminishes as Catherine reforms: 'he acquired a slouching gait, and ignoble look; his naturally reserved disposition was exaggerated into an almost idiotic excess of unsociable moroseness; and he took a grim pleasure, apparently, in exciting the aversion rather than the esteem of his few acquaintance' (p. 68). He is deprived of education, forced to labour, and alienated from Catherine, as she notes in her second diary extract: 'Poor Heathcliff! Hindley calls him a vagabond, and won't let him sit with us, nor eat with us any more; and, he says, he and I must not play together, and threatens to turn him out of the house if we break his orders' (p. 22).

The traumatic consequences of this first separation are clear in Catherine's delirium following the confrontation between Edgar and Heathcliff, which signals a new division from Heathcliff, who will no longer be welcome in Edgar's house. Catherine, driven by desperation, falls back on her final resource:

> Well, if I cannot keep Heathcliff for my friend – if Edgar will be mean and jealous, I'll try to break their hearts by breaking my own. That will be a prompt way of finishing all, when I am pushed to extremity! But it's a deed to be reserved for a forlorn hope – I'd not take Linton by surprise with it. (pp. 116–17)

Nelly sees this as play-acting, because Catherine outlines exactly what she intends to do, but Catherine is in deadly earnest; she is prepared to sacrifice herself, to 'break their hearts by breaking my own', but only as a last resort, as 'a forlorn hope'. If Edgar will be reasonable, and continue to be 'discreet in dreading to provoke me' (p. 117), all will be well. If not, she must take revenge by using the only weapon she now possesses – her own life. Nelly encourages Edgar to resist, and Catherine begins to fulfil her threat by starving herself for three days. Tormented by the thought that Edgar is content in his library while she is dying, she begins to lose all sense of her identity as Catherine Linton. Initially, when she looks into the mirror, she is shocked by her own reflection: 'My God! does he know how I'm altered? [. . .] Is that Catherine Linton?' (p. 121). As she gradually becomes more frenzied, she forgets that she is at Thrushcross Grange, imagining that she is back in her closet-bed at Wuthering Heights. Mistaking the mirror for the black press at the Heights, she thinks the reflection of her face is a ghost: 'It *does* appear odd – I see a face in it! [. . .] Don't *you* see that face? [. . .] Who is it? I hope it will not come out when you are gone! Oh! Nelly, the room is haunted! I'm afraid of being alone!' (p. 123). When Nelly reassures her, 'It was *yourself*, Mrs Linton', she becomes even more terrified: 'Myself [. . .] and the clock is striking twelve! It's true, then; that's dreadful!' (p. 123)

Catherine's distress arises from her complete alienation from the idea of herself as Mrs Linton; in her madness, she has reverted to the episode that keeps being repeated in the novel: her separation from Heathcliff in her twelfth year:

> I'll tell you what I thought, and what has kept recurring and recurring till I feared for my reason – I thought as I lay there with my head against that table leg, and my eyes dimly discerning the grey square of the window, that I was enclosed in the oak-panelled bed at home; and my heart ached with some great grief which, just waking, I could not recollect – I pondered, and worried myself to discover what it could be; and most strangely, the whole last seven years of my life grew a blank! I did not recall that they had been at all. I was a child; my father was just buried, and my misery arose from the separation that Hindley had ordered between me and Heathcliff – I was laid alone, for the first time, and rousing from a dismal doze after a night of weeping – I lifted my hand to push the panels aside, it struck the table-top! I swept it along the carpet, and then, memory burst in – my late anguish was swallowed in a paroxysm of despair – I cannot say why I felt so wildly wretched – it must have been temporary derangement for there is scarcely cause – But, supposing at twelve years old, I had been wrenched from the Heights, and every early association, and my all in all, as Heathcliff was at that time, and been converted at a stroke into Mrs Linton, the lady of Thrushcross Grange, and the wife of a stranger; an exile, and outcast, thenceforth, from what had been my world – You may fancy a glimpse of the abyss where I grovelled! (p. 125)

The turning point in the development of Catherine Earnshaw is not her declaration 'I *am* Heathcliff', which was followed immediately by the loss of her second self at the age of 15, or her marriage to Edgar when she is 17, but the first separation from Heathcliff at 12. She loses more than Heathcliff in this year; Janet Gezari argues that: 'Her identification of herself with Heathcliff, and of her loss of self with loss of him, is grounded in the novel's boldest coincidence; the father's death coincides with the daughter's separation from her companion and bedmate, the older brother's coming into authority, and the onset of the daughter's puberty' (p. 111). Her father's last words to her are 'Why canst thou not always be a good lass, Cathy?', and she never has the opportunity to be properly reconciled to him. She loses her status as daughter of the house, becoming a dependant of her stern older brother, who is clearly set on founding his own family with Frances, a new dynasty which will exclude her. And she is 'wrenched from the Heights, and every early association, and my all in all, as Heathcliff was at that time' by her injury at Thrushcross Grange, which converts her at a stroke into a lady, 'an exile, and outcast, thenceforth, from what had been my world'. Her reversion to her 12-year-old self as Catherine Earnshaw exiles Catherine Linton to a ghost in the black press, or at the window in Lockwood's dream – ' "Catherine Linton," it replied, shiveringly (why did I think of *Linton*? I had read *Earnshaw* twenty times for Linton)' (p. 25). The new Catherine Linton, born from her death, will have to trace her mother's footsteps back to Wuthering Heights before the ghost is laid; it is no coincidence that on her first journey to Wuthering Heights young Catherine Linton is accompanied by a dog called Phenix (p. 194). Catherine Earnshaw's 12-year-old self, 'laid alone, for the first time', will only be appeased when she no longer lies alone: 'I'll not lie there by myself; they may bury me 12 feet deep, and throw the church down over me; but I won't rest till you are with me . . . I never will!' (p. 126).

The final fragmentation of her identity is that between body and spirit. She tells Edgar: 'What you touch at present, you may have; but my soul will be on that hill-top before you lay hands on me again' (p. 128). Her body, her only weapon in the attempt to revenge herself on Heathcliff and Edgar, is now an encumbrance, preventing her from achieving freedom: 'Oh, I'm burning! I wish I were out of doors – I wish I were a girl again, half savage and hardy, and free' (p. 125). She longs for release:

the thing that irks me most is this shattered prison, after all. I'm tired, tired of being enclosed here. I'm wearying to escape into that glorious world, and to be always there; not seeing it dimly through tears, and yearning for it through the walls of an aching heart; but really with it, and in it. (pp. 161–2)

Her body survives merely to fulfil its biological purpose; once she gives birth, she dies. Her body is buried in the open air, in peaty soil that preserves it. If we are to believe Lockwood and Heathcliff, her spirit spends the next 18 years attempting to return to the bed she shared with Heathcliff as a child. Heathcliff wants to sleep in the room, but cannot:

And when I slept in her chamber – I was beaten out of that – I couldn't lie there; for the moment I closed my eyes, she was either outside the window, or sliding back the panels, or entering the room, or even resting her darling head on the same pillow as she did when a child. And I must open my eyes to see. And so I opened and closed them a hundred times a-night – to be always disappointed! It racked me! (p. 290)

Heathcliff eventually dies in this room, lying on the bed with his hand resting on the sill, grazed by the open window (p. 335). It is only when Heathcliff's body is laid next to hers 'to the scandal of the whole neighbourhood' (p. 336) that Catherine, flanked by her 'id' and 'super-ego', Heathcliff and Edgar, is finally complete. Significantly, the spectral figures seen by the little boy are of 'Heathcliff and a woman' (p. 336); Catherine has finally broken free of her childhood and reintegrated with her adult self.

CHAPTER 5

THE THIRD GENERATION

According to Freud, another aspect of the treatment of the 'double' in literature is 'the constant recurrence of the same thing – the repetition of the same features or character traits or vicissitudes, of the same crimes, or even the same names through several consecutive generations' (p. 356). This is exactly what happens in the third generation of *Wuthering Heights*: they replicate the eyes, skin, hair colour and temperament of not just their parents, but their parents' siblings, or long dead ancestors. As J. Hillis Miller notes, even their names do not belong to them: 'Relations of similarity and difference among the characters are indicated by the way several hold the names also held by others or a combination of names held by others. [. . .] Each character in *Wuthering Heights* seems to be an element in a system, defined by his or her place in the system, rather than a separate, unique person' (pp. 56–7). Just as Catherine Earnshaw seems fated to repeat the moment of separation from Heathcliff, the novel's third generation – Hareton Earnshaw, Linton Heathcliff and Catherine Linton – are doomed to repeat not only the physical and psychological traits of previous generations, but also their actions and their sufferings. The three children represent a bizarre experiment in genetic and social engineering, in which Earnshaws, Lintons and Heathcliffs are mixed and matched, debased and elevated, undergoing experiences that are eerily similar to those of Hindley, Catherine, Heathcliff, Edgar and Isabella.

HARETON EARNSHAW

Hareton Earnshaw, 'the last of the ancient Earnshaw stock' (p. 64), bears the name of an earlier ancestor, who had carved his name and the date 1500 over the threshold of Wuthering Heights. Joseph has indoctrinated him with a pride in his heritage and name, and Hareton proclaims to Lockwood: 'My name is Hareton Earnshaw [. . .] and I'd counsel you to respect it!' (p. 14). Yet it is also appropriate, in a novel about the difficulties of interpretation, that this new Hareton is unable to read his own name; deprived of education by Heathcliff, who wants to revenge himself on Hindley by debasing Hindley's son, Hareton has become dissociated from his own identity and social status. His clothes, language and hands mark him out as a common labourer, but there is a dignity in his bearing that confuses Lockwood (pp. 11–12). Hareton's physical traits are entirely Earnshaw. When Nelly sees Hareton for the first time since her move to Thrushcross Grange, she at first thinks the child is an apparition, because he is so similar to Hindley at his age (pp. 109–10). The child Hareton is rough and brutal; he stones Nelly, and his 'baby features' are distorted into 'a shocking expression of malignity' (p. 109). But Hareton differs markedly from Hindley in personality. When Hareton is 18, Nelly is able to see through the Earnshaw features to the mind of the man:

> I thought I could detect in his physiognomy a mind owning better qualities than his father ever possessed. Good things lost amid a wilderness of weeds, to be sure, whose rankness far over-topped their neglected growth; yet notwithstanding, evidence of a wealthy soil that might yield luxuriant crops, under other and favourable circumstances. (p. 196)

The 'wealthy soil' of his mind has been badly neglected, but there is great innate potential in Hareton that Hindley never possessed. Even Heathcliff, who has most to gain from Hareton's degradation, has to admit that he is 'gold put to the use of paving stones' (p. 219).

It is significant that Hareton is most closely associated not with Hindley, but with Catherine and Heathcliff. When Isabella first meets young Hareton, she is struck by 'a look of Catherine in his eyes, and about his mouth' (p. 137). The physical similarity to Catherine becomes more pronounced as Hareton gets older, especially once the neglected soil of his mind begins to be cultivated. He is more like Catherine than her own daughter, and the similarity is so uncanny that Heathcliff finds his desire for revenge thwarted: 'But, when I look for his father in his face, I find *her* every day more! How the devil is he so like?' (p. 303). Hareton emerges as the symbolic child of Catherine and Heathcliff, resembling the one physically, the other in his experiences and the strength of his emotions.

Hareton has been taught to identify much more strongly with his surrogate father, Heathcliff, than with his hated and feared 'Devil daddy' Hindley (p. 109). Heathcliff had rescued him when Hindley dropped him from the banisters (p. 75) (though Nelly claims Heathcliff would have gladly smashed Hareton's skull on the steps to destroy Hindley), and Heathcliff is a powerful ally and weapon for the vulnerable child: 'he pays Dad back what he gies to me – he curses Daddy for cursing me – He says I mun do as I will' (p. 110). Once Hindley is dead, Heathcliff deliberately sets out to replicate his own experience through Hareton: 'Now, my bonny lad, you are *mine*! And we'll see if one tree won't grow as crooked as another, with the same wind to twist it!' (p. 187). It is an experiment in nature and nurture, to see whether Hareton will grow up as bitter, vindictive and intent on revenge against his oppressor as Heathcliff did. But instead of revenging himself on Hindley by destroying his son, Heathcliff condemns himself to relive his own sufferings vicariously through Hareton.

Many of Hareton's actions are deliberately reminiscent of Heathcliff's. When Isabella escapes from the Heights, she knocks over Hareton, who is 'hanging a litter of puppies from a chair back' (p. 183), a symbolic parallel of Heathcliff's hanging of Isabella's dog Fanny on the night of their elopement (p. 150). After Linton's death, Hareton wants to be 'presentable' for young Catherine, and allows Zillah to tidy him up, in exactly the same way that Heathcliff asked Nelly to 'make me decent' for the elder

Catherine (pp. 295, 56). When Hareton strokes Catherine's curl, she reacts as if he had 'stuck a knife into her neck', which is precisely what Heathcliff had done to the fleeing Isabella (pp. 296, 182–3). Most of all, Hareton resembles Heathcliff in his love for young Catherine, who initially makes it clear that it would degrade her even to acknowledge him as her cousin, never mind think of him as a husband. Heathcliff is hypersensitive to Hareton's injured pride and unrequited love, because they are shadows of his own agony in losing Catherine to Edgar: 'I can sympathise with all his feelings, having felt them myself' (p. 219). Heathcliff, who can find nothing of himself in his own son, finds his double in Hareton instead: 'Hareton seemed a personification of my youth, not a human being [. . .]. Hareton's aspect was the ghost of my immortal love, of my wild endeavours to hold my right, my degradation, my pride, my happiness, and my anguish' (pp. 323–4).

Heathcliff's attempt to make him grow crooked fails; Hareton emerges strong, tender and constant. Even Linton affirms: 'Hareton never touches me, he never struck me in his life', in spite of constant provocation (p. 239). Young Catherine treats him with contempt, yet he takes her part and tries to defend her against Heathcliff. Heathcliff and Joseph have taught him to take pride in his brutishness, yet like his father and mother he seems to have an innate desire for civilization and culture. Although practically illiterate, he has secretly collected books, even in Latin and Greek, in an attempt to educate himself, but burns them in mortification and anger when Catherine taunts him:

> He [. . .] gathered the books and hurled them on the fire. I read in his countenance what anguish it was to offer that sacrifice to spleen – I fancied that as they consumed, he recalled the pleasure they had already imparted; and the triumph, and ever increasing pleasure he had anticipated from them – and I fancied I guessed the incitement to his secret studies also. (pp. 302–3)

Catherine is the 'incitement', but Hareton's pleasure in the books for their own sake is genuine, and Nelly rebukes Catherine for mocking him:

had *you* been brought up in his circumstances, would you be less rude? He was as quick and as intelligent a child as ever you were, and I'm hurt that he should be despised now, because that base Heathcliff has treated him so unjustly. (p. 250)

Hareton remains completely loyal to Heathcliff, despite Joseph's mutterings and Catherine's outright defiance, refusing to believe that his surrogate father has malignly usurped his position. Heathcliff boasts to Nelly:

And the best of it is, Hareton is damnably fond of me! [. . .] If the dead villain could rise from his grave to abuse me for his offspring's wrongs, I should have the fun of seeing the said offspring fight him back again, indignant that he should dare to rail at the one friend he has in the world! (p. 219)

Hareton is the only one truly to mourn Heathcliff, sitting all night by the body, pressing his hand, kissing 'the sarcastic, savage face that every one else shrank from contemplating' (p. 335), and digging the sods to cover his grave.

A 'common labourer' at the start of the novel, Hareton ends it as master of Wuthering Heights and prospective master of Thrushcross Grange, which will become his property on his marriage to Catherine. He has been reinstated as a gentleman, has begun the process of becoming educated and socially acceptable and, given Heathcliff's close-handedness, is likely to be quite wealthy. But the marriage also signals the end of the Earnshaws at Wuthering Heights; the newly educated and civilized Hareton will move with Catherine to Thrushcross Grange on New Year's Day 1803, marking both a new beginning and a dramatic rupture with the past.

LINTON HEATHCLIFF

Linton Heathcliff is an abomination, a child conceived and born in hate. Nelly compares him to a 'cockatrice' (p. 275), a mythic animal with a cock's head and a serpent's tail, highlighting the unnatural splicing of Linton and Heathcliff traits in his creation.

His very name is an oxymoron, a reminder of the utter incompatibility of Linton and Heathcliff genes (Miller, p. 57). Linton is an embodiment of the worst aspects of his parents. He is from the outset 'an ailing, peevish creature' (p. 183); none of the Lintons are noted for their physical strength (even Catherine is 'puny' when she is an infant), but Linton takes this to extremes. Even taking his illness into account, he is decadently languorous. His idea of heaven and Catherine's are antithetical:

> He said the pleasantest manner of spending a hot July day was lying from morning till evening on a bank of heath in the middle of the moors, with the bees humming dreamily about among the bloom, and the larks singing high up over head, and the blue sky, and bright sun shining steadily and cloudlessly. That was his most perfect idea of heaven's happiness – mine was rocking in a rustling green tree, with a west wind blowing, and bright, white clouds flitting rapidly above [. . .] but close by great swells of long grass undulating in waves to the breeze; and woods and sounding water, and the whole world awake and wild with joy. He wanted all to lie in an ecstasy of peace; I wanted all to sparkle, and dance in a glorious jubilee. (p. 248)

Linton's heaven, like Linton himself, is 'only half alive' (p. 248).

Like Hareton, Linton most strongly resembles not his parents directly, but a parent's sibling; he has Isabella's eyes, but physically replicates Edgar: 'A pale, delicate, effeminate boy, who might have been taken for my master's younger brother, so strong was the resemblance' (p. 200). Joseph jokes that Edgar must have swapped his daughter for Heathcliff's son, and certainly Catherine Linton has much more energy and physical strength than her cousin, and treats him like a pet: 'He's a pretty little darling when he's good. I'd make such a pet of him, if he were mine' (p. 242). Just as Heathcliff's desire for revenge on Hindley is thwarted by the fact that when he looks at Hareton he sees only Catherine, his triumph in 'seeing *my* descendent [sic] fairly lord of their estates; my child hiring their children, to till their fathers' lands for wages' (p. 208) is destroyed by the fact that when he looks at Linton he sees only Edgar. In spite of his physical dominance, there is no trace of Heathcliff in Linton's appearance; Heathcliff says contemptuously: 'Thou art thy mother's child, entirely! Where is *my* share in thee, puling chicken?' (p. 207)

Linton's physiognomy is superficially good – blond hair, blue eyes, pale skin, graceful carriage – and Edgar reads this as an assurance that his mind is equally acceptable: 'He had a fixed idea [. . .] that as his nephew resembled him in person, he would resemble him in mind' (p. 265). But there are constant reminders that Linton's nature is 'distorted', his character 'defective', and there is more of Heathcliff in him than his face can show (pp. 254, 265). If Hareton can replicate Heathcliff's experiences and emotions, so can Linton. He and young Catherine find two balls in a cupboard, marked 'C' and 'H', clearly balls belonging to the elder Catherine and Heathcliff; Catherine Linton tells Nelly: 'I wished to have the C., because that stood for Catherine, and the H. might be for Heathcliff, his name; but the bran came out of H., and Linton didn't like it' (p. 248). Not only are the two children repeating the childhood play of their parents, but Linton is repeating Heathcliff's dispute with Hindley over the two colts. When Catherine and Linton are forcibly ejected from the room for mocking Hareton, Linton's fury emerges in a powerless attempt to knock down the locked door and hysterical threats against Hareton: 'If you don't let me in I'll kill you! If you don't let me in I'll kill you! [. . .] Devil! devil! I'll kill you, I'll kill you!' Joseph chuckles in recognition: 'Thear, that's t'father! [. . .] That's father! We've allas summat uh orther side in us' (p. 251). This scene repeats the earlier encounter between Linton's father, Heathcliff, and Hareton's father, Hindley, in which Hindley locks Heathcliff out of the Heights, and Heathcliff bursts in to trample Hindley (p. 178), but the new Heathcliff is not physically powerful enough to break down the division to take his revenge on the new Earnshaw.

Linton is terrified of his father, but wishes to emulate his power and aggression; Heathcliff recounts with grim satisfaction: 'I heard him draw a pleasant picture to Zillah of what he would do, if he were as strong as I – the inclination is there, and his very weakness will sharpen his wits to find a substitute for strength'

(p. 288). Linton is incapable of the violence, but longs to inflict his hurt on others from a position of safety: 'He'll undertake to torture any number of cats if their teeth be drawn, and their claws pared' (p. 274). This is reminiscent of Edgar and Isabella's fight over the defenceless puppy, or Isabella's admission 'I'd be glad of a retaliation that wouldn't recoil on myself' (p. 176), reminding the reader that Linton's bad tendencies are inherited from his Linton and Heathcliff ancestors alike.

Linton does not have Hareton's innate qualities – he is 'tin polished to ape a service of silver' (p. 219). But, like the other children in the novel, his faults are exacerbated by the treatment he receives from his father. Barbara Schapiro suggests that: 'He is perhaps the novel's most explicit portrait of that desperate, broken child clamoring beneath the surface of the self – the helpless, needy child which so many of the other characters are trying to defend against' (p. 49). His father makes no effort to conceal his repugnance, going much further than Mr Earnshaw in his rejection of Hindley; Heathcliff inspires a terror in the delicate youth that contributes to his decline: 'my presence is as potent on his nerves, as a ghost; and I fancy he sees me often, though I am not near' (p. 287). Hareton shows some sympathy, but is repelled by Linton's scorn and mockery. Utterly without friends or comfort, Linton's 'bad' nature is made worse, but Brontë makes him reflective enough to understand that he might have been different:

> Papa talks enough of my defects, and shows enough scorn of me, to make it natural I should doubt myself – I doubt whether I am not altogether as worthless as he calls me, frequently; and then I feel so cross and bitter, I hate everybody! I *am* worthless, and bad in temper, and bad in spirit, almost always [. . .] Only, Catherine, do me this justice; believe that if I might be as sweet, and as kind, and as good as you are, I would be, as willingly, and more so, than as happy and as healthy. And, believe that your kindness has made me love you deeper than if I deserved your love, and though I couldn't, and cannot help showing my nature to you, I regret it, and repent it, and shall regret, and repent it, till I die! (pp. 253–4)

Linton has been moulded by his father's contempt and criticism, but recognizes both his own faults and the genuine goodness of Catherine's nature. He sacrifices Catherine to his own fear of his father; he is complicit in her kidnapping and coercion, and repellently complacent at her suffering, refusing to drink his tea because her tears have dropped into it (p. 272). But he does finally help her to escape in spite of his selfishness and terror, and suffers as a result.

CATHERINE LINTON HEATHCLIFF EARNSHAW

Catherine's name epitomizes the compression of identities in the third generation. She is named after her dead mother, but her father calls her Cathy, to make 'a distinction from the mother, and yet, a connection with her'; Edgar had never called his wife Cathy 'probably because Heathcliff had a habit of doing so' (pp. 184–5). So the elder Catherine is Cathy to Heathcliff and Catherine to Edgar; the younger Catherine is Cathy to Edgar and Catherine to Heathcliff. Her maiden name is Catherine Linton, which might seem as much of an oxymoron as Linton Heathcliff, given the decidedly dissimilar characteristics of the Earnshaws and the Lintons, but Catherine has inherited the best, rather than the worst, traits of her parents:

> She was the most winning thing that ever brought sunshine into a desolate house – a real beauty in face – with the Earnshaws' handsome dark eyes, but the Lintons' fair skin, and small features, and yellow curling hair. Her spirits were high, though not rough, and qualified by a heart, sensitive and lively to excess in its affections. That capacity for intense attachments reminded me of her mother; still she did not resemble her; for she could be soft and mild as a dove, and she had a gentle voice, and pensive expression: her anger was never furious; her love never fierce; it was deep and tender. (p. 189)

She has her mother's Earnshaw native energy and emotional depth, but tempered with Linton sensitivity. Her marriage to

Linton translates her into Catherine Heathcliff, an extremely resonant name, associated with the name of the potential self her mother had scratched on the ledge at Wuthering Heights. The elder Catherine had foregone the opportunity to become Catherine Heathcliff; her daughter is compelled to do so. But her new surname links her not only to her mother, but also to her aunt, Isabella Heathcliff: 'Like Isabella she is lured, by Heathcliff's scheming, from the petted and suffocating security of the Grange, and like Isabella she experiences directly the force of his brutality' (Pykett, p. 96). Like Isabella, Catherine is diminished by marriage to a Heathcliff, becoming gloomy and vindictive: 'she seemed to have made up her mind to enter into the spirit of her future family, and draw pleasure from the griefs of her enemies' (p. 288). Her second marriage to Hareton will make her a new Catherine Earnshaw, married to a man who regards Heathcliff as his father, and who has repeated Heathcliff's experiences of dispossession.

Lockwood's first impression of Catherine is that she is, like him, a foreigner in these parts, 'an exotic that the surly indigenae will not recognise for kin' (p. 34); the irony, of course, is that she is living in her mother's childhood home, Wuthering Heights, and should belong there as much as Hareton or Heathcliff. Catherine's 'exotic' qualities have been fostered by isolation; educated at home by her father, until she is 13 she has never been more than a mile from the park of Thrushcross Grange, and never outside on her own, unlike Nelly, Hindley, Heathcliff and the elder Catherine, who roamed the moors from their infancy. Catherine's yearning to visit Penistone Craggs, which seem to her a remote and romantic outpost, is a shadow of her mother's frantic desire to escape from the Grange during her delirium: 'I wish I were out of doors – I wish I were a girl again, half savage and hardy, and free [. . .]. I'm sure I should be myself were I once among the heather on those hills' (pp. 125–6).

Catherine's first escape occurs during Edgar's absence when she is 13. While pretending to be 'an Arabian merchant, going to cross the Desert with his caravan' (p. 192), she makes the expedition to the (to her) equally exotic Wuthering Heights. Just as her mother was attacked by the Lintons' bulldog Skulker on her first illicit visit to the Grange, Catherine is involved in a 'smart battle' with the dogs of the Heights, who injure her dogs Charlie and Phenix (p. 198). When Nelly arrives, it is with a sense of *déjà vu*; Catherine is 'rocking herself in a little chair that had been her mother's, when a child [. . .] perfectly at home', and Hareton is staring at her with the astonishment manifested by the Lintons for Catherine Earnshaw (p. 193). Catherine's stay at the Heights is brief, but transformative; Hareton has not only 'opened the mysteries of the Fairy cave, and twenty other queer places' (p. 198), he has opened her eyes to the complexities of her heritage, and challenged her class assumptions. Like Lockwood, Catherine is puzzled about Hareton's position at the Heights; having discovered that he is not the owner's son, she assumes he must be a servant, and begins to treat him accordingly, ordering him to get her horse, and objecting that he does not show the level of respect and deference that she has come to expect: 'And he never said, Miss; he should have done, shouldn't he, if he's a servant?' (p. 195). When Hareton defies her, she is astonished, and threatens him with the patriarchal power of her father, the former magistrate: 'How dare he speak so to me? Mustn't he be made to do as I ask him? You wicked creature, I shall tell papa what you said – Now then!' (p. 195). Several years later, when Hareton has upset Linton, Catherine threatens to 'tell papa', who would have Hareton 'put in prison, and hanged' (p. 252). For the child Catherine, servants are abject beings with no will of their own, who must 'be made to do as I ask', and those who refuse are 'wicked' and subject to violent retribution. Clearly the major source of Catherine's attitude towards servants and the lower orders is her father, who could never understand his wife's affection for a 'plough-boy', and dealt sternly with servants who refused to accept the elder Catherine's tyranny. Further back, Catherine's grandfather, Mr Linton, was prepared to execute summary justice on Heathcliff on the mere suspicion that he might be a thief (p. 50). Catherine also acts on this paranoid impulse in her treatment of Hareton: 'I gave him a cut with my whip, thinking, perhaps he would murder me' (p. 252).

But the other major influence in young Catherine's life is Nelly, and her reaction to Hareton's defiance of Catherine is telling:

'There, Miss Cathy! you see you have got into pretty company [. . .]. Nice words to be used to a young lady!' (p. 195). In spite of her sympathy for her first nursling, Nelly blames Hareton, and reinforces Catherine's indoctrination that 'a young lady' should keep to 'pretty company', and should encounter only 'Nice words'. It is not Nelly who rebukes Catherine for her haughtiness, but Heathcliff's housekeeper, who points out that she was never hired to serve Catherine, and Hareton is not a servant but Catherine's equal, in fact her cousin. Catherine's horror at the idea of her relationship to Hareton demonstrates how intrinsic class is to her sense of identity. Ironically, she insists that her cousin is 'a gentleman's son', ignorant that the cousin she is pre-pared to acknowledge (Linton) is the son of a nameless outcast, while the cousin she rejects (Hareton) is descended from one of the oldest and most respected families in the area.

Catherine's next visit to the Heights, at the age of 16, also has the quality of repetition. She has been caught by Heathcliff 'plundering, or, at least, hunting out the nests of the grouse' on Heights land (p. 214). There is a curious echo here, obviously of Heathcliff and Catherine's trespass onto Grange land, but also of the elder Catherine's memory of the lapwing on the moor during her illness: 'we saw its nest in the winter, full of little skeletons. Heathcliff set a trap over it, and the old ones dare not come. I made him promise he'd never shoot a lapwing, after that, and he didn't' (pp. 122–3). Once again Catherine tries to place Hareton, asking Heathcliff 'Is he your son?', and once again she expects to be treated with respect because of her father; when Heathcliff asks who 'papa' is, she replies: 'Mr Linton of Thrushcross Grange [. . .]. I thought you did not know me, or you wouldn't have spoken in that way' (p. 214). Just as her mother is set apart from Heathcliff by the Lintons as soon as they recognize her as Earnshaw's daughter, so Catherine expects to be exonerated of the suspicion of plunder as soon as she is known to be Edgar Linton's daughter, and therefore above reproach.

Just as her mother develops a 'double character' (p. 67) o ₁ her return from the Grange, attempting to keep up her old rel ₁tion-ship with Heathcliff while encouraging the new one wiᵼh the Lintons, so Catherine finds herself mired in duplicity in her attempt to maintain contact with Linton in spite of her father's wishes that she break off all communication with Heathcliff's family. Their courtship takes place on the page rather than in person, in the exchange of books and notes. Catherine's 'play-things' and 'trinkets' are 'transmuted into bits of folded paper' that she hoards in a special drawer (p. 224). If, as Gilbert and Gubar suggest, Edgar's power resides in his mastery of books and documents (p. 281), Catherine's changing relationship with books is symptomatic of her precarious access to power. Initially, her books are a form of currency; she bribes the groom Michael with books to help her get to the Heights while Edgar and Nelly are ill, and when imprisoned by Heathcliff offers Linton her books if he will free her. Linton covets her books; Catherine says: 'his books are not as nice as mine, and he wanted to have them extremely, when I told him how interesting they were' (p. 223–4). Catherine's investment in Linton's letters leaves her vulnerable; whereas before she was the plunderer of nests, now she is metaphorically transformed into a bird whose nest of letters is plundered by Nelly:

> Never did any bird flying back to a plundered nest which it had left brim-ful of chirping young ones, express more com-plete despair in its anguished cries, and flutterings, than she by her single 'Oh!' and the change that transfigured her late happy countenance. (p. 226)

Once she is married, Catherine's changed relationship to books signals her loss of power; her books are now her husband's prop-erty, and she cannot use them to bargain, as Linton makes clear: 'I told her she had nothing to give, they were all, all mine' (p. 280). Following Linton's death, Heathcliff destroys her books, which he regards as 'trash' and 'idle tricks', in order to force her to earn her keep (p. 30). Catherine is so dependent on reading for consolation that she is even prepared to try 'Joseph's store of the-ology' (p. 301), which had been rejected so violently by her mother and Heathcliff. Unlike her mother, who uses the margins and blanks of these religious texts as her diary, Catherine cannot even subvert the legitimate purpose of these books: 'I have no materials for writing, not even a book from which I might tear a leaf' (p. 300). Books are both 'treasures' which she has been robbed of and sacred objects to Catherine, and she resents most Hareton's appropriation of her favourite texts: 'Those books, both prose and verse, were consecrated to me by other associations, and I hate to have them debased and profaned in his mouth!' (p. 302). Just as Heathcliff's education is suddenly stopped by Hindley, and he falls behind Catherine, young Catherine fears that Hareton will profit by her books while her mind stagnates.

Her intermittent access to and control over books is symptomatic of her general lack of power as a woman in a patriarchal society. As Heathcliff points out, the 'young chit has no expectations' (p. 215); she cannot inherit Thrushcross Grange because her grandfather's will stipulates it will go to a male heir. Edgar has set aside money for Catherine's 'fortune', the money she will bring to a future husband, in an attempt to secure her future in the only way that is possible to women of her class and time – marriage. But he longs for Catherine to be able to stay in 'the house of her ancestors', and the only way this will be possible is if she marries his heir, Linton (p. 259). Linton crows: 'Catherine always spoke of it as *her* house. It isn't hers! It's mine – papa says everything she has is mine' (p. 280). Even after Linton's death she is unable to inherit, because Heathcliff has forced Linton to leave his possessions to him, and as Nelly notes: 'I suppose legally, at any rate Catherine, destitute of cash and friends, cannot disturb his possession' (p. 294). Catherine would only have been able to make a claim in court through a male relative, and her closest male relative now is her father-in-law, Heathcliff. Catherine is entirely dependent on the man who hates her as the cause of her mother's death, and her only hope is a second marriage which will remove her from his power. As Zillah points out, Catherine's 'learning' and 'daintiness' are entirely useless, and she has been left worse off than any servant: 'She's as poor as you, or I – poorer – I'll be bound – you're saving – and I'm doing my little, all that road' (p. 295).

Catherine's return to power and the Grange is achieved through books, but only once she has renounced her pride and asked forgiveness. She reconciles with Hareton over one of the books Nelly has smuggled from the Grange, and teaches him to read, just as her mother had tried to help Heathcliff by teaching him what she learnt while Heathcliff was deprived of education (p. 46). As Lyn Pykett points out: 'Catherine's civilising of Hareton is an interesting variant of a common scene in eighteenth- and nineteenth-century fiction in which a male character offers improving reading to an "ignorant" (but improvable) female' (p. 83). Catherine's knowledge is power, and instead of abandoning the man she loves to marry someone more appropriate, which is what her mother did, she is able to mould the man she loves into a suitable partner, tugging his hair and slapping his cheek when he fails, kissing him when he succeeds (p. 307). Heathcliff's death frees Catherine; when Lockwood returns to the Grange to settle his tenancy, Nelly tells him 'it is with Mrs Heathcliff you must settle' (p. 309), but she is still not entirely in control. Nelly acts as Catherine's business agent, as 'She has not learnt to manage her affairs yet' (p. 309), and Catherine's impending marriage to Hareton will probably mean that she never will; as Torgerson notes: 'the novel closes prior to Catherine's second experience of being dispossessed of her land, her name, her legal rights, her power. Hareton, not Catherine, will own the land where Catherine was born' (p. 122). But she has, of course, achieved freedom of a sort, symbolized by her physical liberation; in her childhood she was confined to the Grange, following her marriage to Linton she was a prisoner at the Heights, but now Nelly has to scold her for the 'late rambles' she and Hareton take on the moors every evening (p. 309).

Lockwood's last view of the lovers is as they halt on the door-stones of Wuthering Heights, under the name Hareton Earnshaw and the date 1500, to 'take a last look at the moon, or, more correctly, at each other, by her light' (p. 337). It is a nineteenth-century literary convention to end a novel with a marriage, and Brontë to an extent bends to the convention in offering the prospective love-match of Hareton and Catherine. But it is not an unmitigated or unambiguous happy ending; the union of the young lovers is overshadowed by the speculative, spectral reunion of Heathcliff and Catherine, and the abandonment of the ancestral home of the Earnshaws. Catherine is about to become a new Catherine Earnshaw, but she will raise the next generation of Earnshaws in enclosed isolation at Thrushcross Grange, the home of her Linton ancestors.

THROUGH THE CHARACTERS TO THE KEY THEMES AND ISSUES

Charlotte Brontë described her sister Emily as a 'nominal artist', never fully in control of her material, working passively under the dictation of 'Fate' or 'Inspiration', and *Wuthering Heights* as a work of art 'hewn in a wild workshop, with simple tools, out of homely materials' (p. liv). In fact, *Wuthering Heights* is an incredibly sophisticated novel: it is so carefully planned that it is possible to date every incident in the plot with great accuracy, and even relatively minor characters are fleshed out with convincing idiosyncratic traits. One thing that becomes clear in an analysis of the characters of *Wuthering Heights* is that no character, not even the charismatic and enigmatic Catherine and Heathcliff, can be fully comprehended in isolation. The repetition of traits and fates through three generations of Earnshaws, Lintons and Heathcliffs is grounded in both Brontë's understanding of contemporary scientific and psychological facts, and in her appreciation of the Gothic 'uncanny', in which doubles, troubling ancestral homes, mouldering graves, spectres and nightmares abound. The same names, faces, bodies and voices are recycled in such an evident and over-determined way that critics have been led to suggest that there are no characters in *Wuthering Heights* because no single character is unique. Individuals dissolve into each other, as Heathcliff hopes to do with Catherine after his death, finally achieving physically the sense of oneness they both express in life.

But Brontë demonstrates the difference in similarity: Edgar Linton and Linton Heathcliff may look strikingly similar, but they are not the same; Hareton Earnshaw and Heathcliff undergo the same disappointments and trials, but react very differently. Catherine Linton, born from her mother's death, inherits her mother's eyes and voice, and in her marriage to Hareton resurrects her mother's original identity as Catherine Earnshaw. Yet she shows almost no interest in her dead mother; when Linton discovers the locket she wears, containing pictures of her mother and father, Catherine breaks the hinges and offers him the picture of her mother if he will let her keep her beloved father's image (pp. 280–1). The physical and legal identities of individuals – their bodies and their names, which are so evidently repeated – are not the only things that constitute character; the minds and hearts of the characters are formed chiefly from their childhood experiences.

The characters of *Wuthering Heights* are, of course, literary constructs, vehicles of meaning which Brontë uses to elaborate on various ideas and issues. The wealth of detail in the characterization lends the novel to a multitude of potential theoretical interpretations. For example, a Marxist reading might examine both the extent to which the novel is a product of Victorian capitalist values, and the way in which characters such as Hindley, Heathcliff, Catherine, Edgar and Hareton are shaped by those values in their desire to achieve or maintain social position, education, and wealth. Catherine and Heathcliff may be read as revolutionary figures, subverting the conventional appropriative principles and financial anxieties of their forebears; but they can also be seen as essentially conformist figures who absorb these principles and anxieties and act accordingly – Catherine in her marriage to the eminently suitable Edgar, Heathcliff in his accumulation of property and wealth at the expense of others.

A feminist interpretation of the novel might consider whether *Wuthering Heights* was a challenge to or a reinforcement of the discourse of patriarchy in the Victorian period. Brontë published the novel under a pseudonym, Ellis Bell, which suggests her awareness that *Wuthering Heights* and its characters would be read very differently by a contemporary audience if they were known to be the creations of a female artist. Charlotte Brontë said that she and her sisters chose pseudonyms that were not 'positively masculine', but that certainly left their gender ambiguous:

> we did not like to declare ourselves women, because – without at that time suspecting that our mode of writing and thinking was not what is called 'feminine' – we had a vague impression that authoresses are liable to be looked on with prejudice [. . .] (p. xliv)

The narrative structure emphasizes the dominance of men over women in giving precedence to Lockwood, whose text encloses and comments on that of Nelly. In the two Catherines and Isabella, Brontë offers compelling instances of women who are dispossessed, coerced, goaded and physically attacked by patriarchal figures such as Mr Linton, Heathcliff and even the seemingly gentle Edgar.

An historicist reading could focus on the ways in which the characters of *Wuthering Heights* are situated in a specific place and time – the north of England in the late eighteenth and very early nineteenth centuries – reflecting on the key historical events that are embedded in the chronology of the text or the time of writing: the American War of Independence, the Act of Union or the Great Famine, for instance. A postcolonial critic would examine the literal and metaphorical references to slavery, colonization and racial difference, particularly with reference to Heathcliff. However, as J. Hillis Miller has argued, there is no 'single, unified, and logically coherent' meaning in *Wuthering Heights*, and an attempt to approach the novel from only one perspective will inevitably overlook its rich complexity and diversity (p. 51). Close attention to the characters, shaped as they are by powerful internal and external forces, allows us access to the multiplicity of ideas, images, themes and symbols that congregate in Emily Brontë's one and only novel.

GUIDE TO FURTHER READING

BIOGRAPHY AND CONTEXT

Barker, Juliet (1995), *The Brontës*. London: Phoenix. Indispensable biography of the Brontë family.

Barker, Juliet (1997), *The Brontës: A Life in Letters*. London: Viking. Few of Emily's letters remain, but this contains the diary papers Emily wrote with her sister Anne.

Brontë, Charlotte (2003), 'Biographical notice of Ellis and Acton Bell' and 'Editor's preface to the new [1850] edition of Wuthering Heights', in Emily Brontë, *Wuthering Heights*, ed. Pauline Nestor (revised edn). London: Penguin. Very important reading for the way in which Charlotte attempted to protect and manipulate her sister's reputation after Emily's death.

Ingham, Patricia (2006), *Authors in Context: The Brontës*. Oxford: Oxford University Press. An excellent introduction to the context, with chapters on biography, society, the literary context, social class, gender, nationality and race, the psyche, religion and adaptations.

CRITICISM

There are several extremely useful collections of critical essays from the earliest reviews to more recent responses. These include:

Allott, Miriam (ed.) (1987), *Wuthering Heights: A Casebook*. Basingstoke and London: Macmillan. Several essays particularly useful for characterization, such as Van Ghent's 'Dark "Otherness"' and Allott's 'The Rejection of Heathcliff?'.

Bloom, Harold (ed.) (1993), *Major Literary Characters: Heathcliff.* New York and Philadelphia: Chelsea House Publishers. Short extracts from early critical perspectives, followed by longer essays representing more recent readings. Despite the title, many of the extracts and essays are not specific to Heathcliff, ranging over the novel more generally.

Dunn, Richard J. (ed.) (2003), *Wuthering Heights: The 1847 Text: Backgrounds and Contexts; Criticism* (4th edn). New York and London: W. W. Norton & Co. Very useful biographical and contextual information, followed by essays from a wide range of theoretical perspectives.

Stoneman, Patsy (ed.) (2000), *Emily Brontë: Wuthering Heights: A Reader's Guide to Essential Criticism.* Cambridge: Icon Books. Extracts from essential criticism from 1848 to the late twentieth century; an excellent overview of prevailing ideas, and the evolution of criticism of the novel.

The following critical texts contain very useful chapters on, or references to, *Wuthering Heights*:

Eagleton, Terry (1975), *Myths of Power: A Marxist Study of the Brontës.* London and Basingstoke: Macmillan. Concentrates on Charlotte, but contains an important chapter on *Wuthering Heights*, demonstrating the ways in which Heathcliff internalizes the bourgeois values of the Lintons and Earnshaws in order to destroy them.

Gezari, Janet (2007), *Last Things: Emily Brontë's Poems.* Oxford and New York: Oxford University Press. Some fascinating reflections on the connections between Brontë's Gondal poetry and *Wuthering Heights*.

Gilbert, Sandra and Susan Gubar (2000), *The Madwoman in the Attic: The Woman Writer and the Nineteenth-Century Literary Imagination* (2nd edn). New Haven and London: Yale University Press. Influential feminist reading of the novel in the chapter 'Looking oppositely: Emily Brontë's Bible of hell'.

Glen, Heather (ed.) (2002), *The Cambridge Companion to the Brontës*. Cambridge: Cambridge University Press. Useful collection of recent critical essays on the Brontës, including Stevie Davies on the connections between *Wuthering Heights, The Professor* and *Agnes Grey*, and Rick Rylance on ideology and personality in the novels.

Meyer, Susan (1996), *Imperialism at Home: Race and Victorian Women's Fiction*. Ithaca and London: Cornell University Press. Good overview of the use of race as a metaphor in Victorian literature. Contains a chapter on 'Reverse imperialism in *Wuthering Heights*', and the chapters on Charlotte Brontë's African tales and her novel *Jane Eyre* are also useful contextually.

Miller, J. Hillis (1982), *Fiction and Repetition: Seven English Novels*. Oxford: Basil Blackwell. A reading of novels by Conrad, Thackeray, Hardy, Woolf and Brontë. The chapter on '*Wuthering Heights*: repetition and the uncanny' focuses on the novel's resistance to interpretation.

Pykett, Lyn (1989), *Women Writers: Emily Brontë*. Basingstoke and London: Macmillan. Important feminist reading, demonstrating the way the novel breaks the boundaries between genres such as the Gothic and domestic realism.

Taylor, Jenny Bourne and Sally Shuttleworth (eds) (1998), *Embodied Selves: An Anthology of Psychological Texts 1830–1890*. Oxford: Clarendon Press. A fascinating collection of extracts from Victorian scientific texts with introductions outlining Victorian psychological theories.

BIBLIOGRAPHY

PRIMARY TEXT

Brontë, Emily (2003), *Wuthering Heights*, ed. Pauline Nestor (revised edn). London: Penguin.

SECONDARY TEXTS

Allott, Miriam (ed.) (1987), *Wuthering Heights: A Casebook*. Basingstoke and London: Macmillan.

Baldridge, Cates (1988), 'Voyeuristic rebellion: Lockwood's dream and the reader of *Wuthering Heights*'. *Studies in the Novel*, 20 (3), 274–87.

Barker, Juliet (1995), *The Brontës*. London: Phoenix.

Barker, Juliet (1997), *The Brontës: A Life in Letters*. London: Viking.

Bloom, Harold (ed.) (1993), *Major Literary Characters: Heathcliff*. New York and Philadelphia: Chelsea House Publishers.

Botting, Fred (ed.) (1988), *New Casebooks: Frankenstein*. Basingstoke and New York: Palgrave.

Brontë, Charlotte (2003), 'Biographical notice of Ellis and Acton Bell' and 'Editor's preface to the new [1850] edition of Wuthering Heights', in Emily Brontë, *Wuthering Heights*, ed. Pauline Nestor (revised edn). London: Penguin.

Byron, Lord George (1986), *The Oxford Authors: Byron*, ed. Jerome J. McGann. Oxford and New York: Oxford University Press.

Davies, Stevie (1994), *Emily Brontë: Heretic*. London: The Women's Press.

Dunn, Richard J. (ed.) (2003), *Wuthering Heights: The 1847 Text: Backgrounds and Contexts; Criticism* (4th edn). New York and London: W. W. Norton & Co.

Eagleton, Terry (1975), *Myths of Power: A Marxist Study of the Brontës*. London and Basingstoke: Macmillan.

Eagleton, Terry (1995), *Heathcliff and the Great Hunger: Studies in Irish Culture*. London and New York: Verso.

Freud, Sigmund (1990), *Art and Literature*, ed. James Strachey. Harmondsworth: Penguin.

Gargano, Elizabeth (2000), 'The intersection of text and dream: a palimsestic reading of Lockwood's nightmare visions in *Wuthering Heights*'. *Topic*, 50, 77–90.

Gérin, Winifred (1971), *Emily Brontë: A Biography*. Oxford: Clarendon Press.

Gezari, Janet (2007), *Last Things: Emily Brontë's Poems*. Oxford and New York: Oxford University Press.

Gilbert, Sandra and Susan Gubar (2000), *The Madwoman in the Attic: The Woman Writer and the Nineteenth-Century Literary Imagination* (2nd edn). New Haven and London: Yale University Press.

Glen, Heather (ed.) (2002), *The Cambridge Companion to the Brontës*. Cambridge: Cambridge University Press.

Holbrook, David (1997), *Wuthering Heights: A Drama of Being*. Sheffield: Sheffield Academic Press.

Ingham, Patricia (2006), *Authors in Context: The Brontës*. Oxford: Oxford University Press.

Leavis, Q. D. (1993), 'A fresh approach to *Wuthering Heights*', in Patsy Stoneman (ed.), *New Casebooks: Wuthering Heights*. Basingstoke and London: Macmillan.

Marsh, Nicholas (1999), *Analysing Texts: Emily Brontë, Wuthering Heights*. Basingstoke and London: Macmillan.

McLemore, Joy Ellis (1981), 'Edgar Linton: master of Thrushcross Grange'. *RE: Artes Liberales*, 8 (3), 13–26.

Meyer, Susan (1996), *Imperialism at Home: Race and Victorian Women's Fiction*. Ithaca and London: Cornell University Press.

Miller, J. Hillis (1982), *Fiction and Repetition: Seven English Novels*. Oxford: Basil Blackwell.

Milton, John (1971), *Paradise Lost*, ed. Alastair Fowler. London and New York: Longman.

Mitchell, Hayley R. (ed.) (1999), *Readings on Wuthering Heights*. San Diego: Greenhaven Press.

Paris, Bernard J. (1997), *Imagined Human Beings: A Psychological Approach to Character and Conflict in Literature*. New York and London: New York University Press.

Pykett, Lyn (1989), *Women Writers: Emily Brontë*. Basingstoke and London: Macmillan.

Ratchford, Fannie (1964), *The Brontës' Web of Childhood* (re-issued edn). New York: Russell & Russell.

Schapiro, Barbara (1989), 'The rebirth of Catherine Earnshaw: splitting and reintegration of self in *Wuthering Heights*'. *Nineteenth Century Studies*, 3, 37–51.

Shakespeare, William (1998), *Twelfth Night*, eds Roger Warren and Stanley Wells. Oxford: Oxford University Press.

Shuttleworth, Sally (1996), *Charlotte Brontë and Victorian Psychology*. Cambridge: Cambridge University Press.

Stoneman, Patsy (ed.) (2000), *Emily Brontë: Wuthering Heights: A Reader's Guide to Essential Criticism*. Cambridge: Icon Books.

Taylor, Jenny Bourne (1988), *In the Secret Theatre of Home: Wilkie Collins, Sensation Narrative, & Nineteenth-Century Psychology*. London and New York: Routledge.

Taylor, Jenny Bourne and Sally Shuttleworth (eds) (1998), *Embodied Selves: An Anthology of Psychological Texts 1830–1890*. Oxford: Clarendon Press.

Thaden, Barbara Z. (2001), *Student Companion to Charlotte and Emily Brontë*. Westport and London: Greenwood Press.

Thomas, Ronald R. (1990), *Dreams of Authority: Freud and the Fictions of the Unconscious*. Ithaca and London: Cornell University Press.

Torgerson, Beth (2005), *Reading the Brontë Body: Disease, Desire, and the Contraints of Culture*. Basingstoke and New York: Palgrave Macmillan.

Van Ghent, Dorothy (1987), 'Dark "Otherness" in *Wuthering Heights*', in Miriam Allott (ed.), *Wuthering Heights: A Casebook*. Basingstoke and London: Macmillan.

Wilde, Oscar (2000), *The Importance of Being Earnest and Other Plays*, ed. Richard Allen Cave. London: Penguin.

Wilson, A. N. (2002), *The Victorians*. London: Hutchinson.

Wordsworth, William (1984), *The Oxford Authors: William Wordsworth*, ed. Stephen Gill. Oxford and New York: Oxford University Press.

INDEX